MONEY
MASTERY

Making Sense of Making Money
for Making a Difference

BILLY EPPERHART, M.B.A.

Harrison House

SHIPPENSBURG, PA

CONTENTS

LETTER FROM BILLY EPPERHART

Baking 101: When making something as simple as pancakes from scratch, it is important to have all the right ingredients in the proper amounts. Without the correct measurements, something is bound to go wrong. And without all the ingredients, well, you don't get quite what you're expecting.

One morning, I decided to surprise my wife, Becky, with home-made pancakes. I purchased all of the ingredients the day before, and while Becky slept, I snuck into the kitchen. I whipped up the batter, heated up the pan, and coated it with butter. I was quietly zooming around the kitchen and felt the relief sink in as I started pouring the batter into the pan. I was going to pull this off! But then I noticed that my pancakes weren't rising. Instead of fluffy, soft pancakes, I had thin, hard teacup plates.

When you have an intuitive, strong woman at your side, you quickly learn that it's hard to pull off surprises. Becky awoke, walked in the kitchen, and found me puzzling over the mess. Without a moment's hesitation she asked, "Did you forget the baking soda?"

My head snapped to the counter where, sure enough, the orange box of baking soda sat unopened. I had tried my best to surprise her (and I guess in some way I had), but I was disappointed. We pressed on though, so instead of eating china plates for breakfast, I took her out for a wonderful morning date. By the way, the restaurant used baking soda in its pancakes.

The key to this innocent story is the missing ingredient. Too often in the U.S., we are told that God wants us to prosper, yet nobody is telling us how to prosper. Instead of choosing God as our only master, we choose money. In other words, we are mastered by our money.

Over the years, as I worked as an entrepreneur and investor, I prayed a lot about finances. And through working with God, He gave me the missing ingredient— The Triple X Factor. The Triple X Factor is the key to making the metaphorical pancakes in your life rise. It shifts your position relating to money from being mastered to mastering. It puts you in a place of wealth where you can give back. When you partner with God in this process, you are able to reach a place of investing deeply in the kingdom.

My heart in writing this book is to teach you how to break the hold money has over your life so that you can be free to serve God. How awesome would it be to have all you need and, according to 2 Corinthians 9, "be able to give to every good cause!" That's a good place to be.

When I talk about "Money Mastery," I'm talking about you and me becoming the masters of our money as we serve God. Through this book, I hope to finally commit to paper some of the most important lessons I've learned along the path of wealth building. I pray that you are encouraged and equipped to reach new levels of wealth—not for the purpose of building bigger barns for yourself—for the purpose of maintaining your barns and investing in the Kingdom of God.

The teaching in this book is as practical as it is spiritual, and throughout it, I will provide know-how, experience and tools to empower you to become financially free. I will also give you the scriptural foundation for why and how you should steward your wealth appropriately. All you have to do is prayerfully take action and move forward!

Blessings,

Billy

DEDICATION

I dedicate this book to my beautiful wife of 45 years, Becky. I also dedicate this book to my daughter, Brooke, my son, Brant, his wife, Abi, and my four grandsons, Brayden, Nolan, Camden, and Owen.

ACKNOWLEDGMENTS

Thank you to Amanda for the many, many hours of writing and editing to make this book a possibility. I pray every day for divine connections, and Amanda has been one.

I also want to thank Andrew Wommack, Paul Milligan, Charis Bible College and Charis Business School for the opportunities to develop and expand my teaching and ideas. I'm convinced that Charis Business School is the best place you can go for a Kingdom-minded business education.

PART ONE:
BAKING SODA
AND THE BASICS

CHAPTER ONE:

UNDERSTANDING WEALTH

No one can serve two masters. Either you will hate the one and love the other, or you will be devoted to the one and despise the other. You cannot serve both God and money.

—Matthew 6:24 (NIV)

Jesus made it plain when He said, "You cannot serve both God and money." Yet many people serve money without ever making a conscious choice to do so. By not learning how to manage our money, we become servants to our finances. So many of us have a heart that wants to boldly serve God, but we end up serving money by default—simply because of our situation in life.

As we learn how to manage and control our finances, we will start mastering our money. And the thing that I like the most is that in the process of Money Mastery, it becomes possible to learn how to *make* money. We can learn how to cause an increase of finances in our lives so that we can fully serve God.

I remember the first time I realized I didn't have to think about my monthly or annual budget. It was a freeing experience. Now I'm not saying that I don't ever have to manage money; I just no longer have to think about whether or not I'm going to make it from week to week or month to month or, for that matter, year to year.

The best part of mastering my money is that I now have so much more time to focus on true riches that are only found in God. I also have the financial freedom to turn around and immediately do what God says. It's wonderful! And it's not impossible to get there. Anyone can do this!

THE MIDDLE MAN

Money is a representative of a certain quantity of corn or other commodity. It is so much warmth, so much bread.

—Ralph Waldo Emerson

If we're going to learn how to master money, we first need to define and understand what money is. So what is money? In simple terms, money is the *middle man*. I love this quote by Emerson: Money is really just a representative of other things. It is corn, movie night and diamond rings.

In reality, money replaces the need for us to carry around chickens and bushels of apples to buy things. Thankfully, we don't have to bring a quarter of a cow to the grocery store today to buy our Thanksgiving meal. We have this freedom because money acts as the currency in the middle. In its truest sense, money is our medium of exchange. We don't get paid for work (at least in the U.S.) in the form of apples or chickens; we get paid in the form of money—and that's a good thing!

Money is also a representation of what we trade for our time and value. We work; we get paid. In other words, we put our life's energy into our work, and in return, we receive money. Money is also the standard placed on the value of items. Therefore, we are able to take an item and assign it a dollar sign with a specific amount attached to it. This tells us what the item *costs* and more importantly, what the item is *worth*.

I think when we put money in this light, we can suddenly see how it's not really that big of a deal. It's not something that much emotion should be directed toward. Loving or hating money is neither here nor there. It's what we do with money that becomes worth talking about.

THE GOOD SAMARITAN'S RESOURCES

No one would remember the Good Samaritan if he only had good intentions, he had money as well.

—Margaret Thatcher, UK Prime Minister

Sometimes we want to do good for God—or for people or for other things—but we are hindered by our lack of resources. If we don't have any resources, we're stuck. As Thatcher said, the Good Samaritan didn't just have good intentions, he had resources that empowered him to take care of a person in need. We should have that same goal in mind when we seek to obtain more resources.

Years ago, I was on vacation with my wife in Hong Kong, and we stayed at an amazing spa. I'm telling you, it was beautiful. Our deck looked overlooked Victoria Harbor, and it was close enough to the shore that we could hear the lapping of the waves.

During our stay, I found an old bookstore. I began thumbing through random books and came across this quote by Felix Dennis:

"I was put on earth to get rich, to collect the money that already had my name on it, and then give it all away." *Wow*, was all I could think!

The Law of Connection, which we'll talk about later, says that God has a treasure chest of divine connections for each person. These divine connections are Kairos moments or God-opportune moments. Finding this quote in Hong Kong was a divine connection for me.

> **And my God shall supply all your need according to His riches in glory by Christ Jesus.**
>
> Philippians 4:19

I believe God has prepared a great capacity for every person on this planet. We each have a purpose on this earth. We also have resources and money out there that God has readied for us. He has a treasure chest of divine connections for each one of us, and the Bible makes it clear that God is no respecter of persons (Acts 10:34). He will do for one what He will do for another.

When we see people with great resources and remember that God is no respecter of persons, it means that there are great resources out there for anyone. If there are resources for Billy, there are resources for you. Somewhere in the world, there is money with your name on it. And I don't know about you, but if it's got my name on it and God put it there for me, I'm going after it!

Everything, however, hinges on the last part of this quote: "And then give it all away." It's not about heaping wealth upon ourselves, right? It's not just about us having barns. In Luke 12, we see that it's okay for us to have some barns, but it's not okay to build bigger barns. Of course, God wants us to have resources; He wants us to be blessed. But the idea is that we are blessed so that we can be a blessing. (Genesis 12:2)

I will give you the treasures of darkness and hidden riches of secret places, that you may know that I, the Lord, who calls you by your name, am the God of Israel.

Isaiah 45:3

Notice that it says, "the hidden riches of secret places." There are some hidden riches in secret places. This means that there's some money out there that has your name on it!

As we dive deeper into this book, I'm going to reveal some nuances, or what I like to call "secret sauce" to finding these riches that God has for us. I believe there's money out there with your name on it, and there's no reason for the world or the wicked to have it all. I found the money with my name on it, and now I'm at a place where I can give it away.

I want to help you get to that place also. I want you to open your eyes and see "the hidden riches of secret places". It's time for the body of Christ to let the eyes of our understanding be unveiled so we are able to see, understand, and know that we can be the masters of our money!

MY MONEY MASTERY STORY

I actually have a bit of a different story when it comes to Money Mastery. My background is primarily as a minister, but from the very beginning, I never looked at pastoring as a career per se. Instead, I always owned investment real estate and had a couple of properties on hand.

When I was a much younger man, the church I pastored was hosting a major conference. By major, I mean that we had seven private jets on the runway. There were some hitters in the house! These guest speakers flew in on private jets their ministries owned.

When the conference was over, two of the guys—who flew in on their own planes— and I went to the mountains for a couple of days of R&R. We went to a huge hot springs pool in the mountains of Colorado. As we stood in the heated water, which was a little less than waist deep, one of the guys looked at me and said, "Billy, what kind of plans have you made for retirement?"

Usually, a conversation would start with, "So, did you enjoy the drive up?" or "What did you think about the conference?" But this guy just jumped right in and asked me what kind of plans I had for retirement. I thought about my real estate investment and what little money I had put aside, but before I could respond, he said something that shook me to my core. He said, "If I did not have my ministry, I would be broke in 90 days. I would literally be out on the street."

That terrified me! At the time, I was aspiring to be one of these men who had flown in on their ministry's jets. That was my goal! I had a little investment real estate and had set aside a small amount of money, but I was mostly focusing on growing and building my ministry. So when he said that, I believe it was one of those divine connections God had stored in a treasure chest for me. God showed up in my life that day and began to show me something I had not yet understood.

When I returned home from that R&R trip, I began a journey. I was determined to replace all of my salary and benefits with passive income—income I didn't have to work for. At the time, my salary, benefits and travel felt like a pretty big paycheck, so that was a significant goal for me to try to reach. But I was determined. So I set my face like a flint, and here's what happened.

By God's grace, I caught the real estate market at just the right time in the U.S. During this time, I was developing and practicing the formulas that I now teach in my Real Estate Mastery course. I was learning how not to overpay for real estate. After the first ten properties and over the course of two and a half years, I finally reached my goal of replacing my income with passive income. I didn't have to sell something or put in X hours to collect this extra income.

I remember the specific day I replaced my salary and benefits with passive income. It was a monumental moment for me! I was sitting in the parking lot in front of a Starbucks, enjoying a Quad Grande Americano—no cream, no sugar. It's what I call a "man's man's drink." As I was sitting there, I received a call from one of my property managers and my accountant. In those days, as I began to grow and expand, I had six property managers and one accountant.

This particular manager was handling a lot of property at the time, and told me we had reached my goal. I had replaced all of my income with passive income. Suddenly I felt so *free,* and on that day, I truly became the master of my money!

In my mind, what I was doing was meaningful but here's the thing: Everything I did back then in reaching that goal, I did totally for myself. My reasons were entirely selfish. I wasn't thinking about how I could serve God with my money. I simply did this so I could be financially free.

At that time, I didn't understand God's purpose or plan for my life. I had no idea that God was using that selfish period in my life to move me toward something special. But later, I began to see God's true purpose. God knew the plans He had for me; He knew that I had a hope and a future. And I thank God for that! I thank God that He knew more than I did in the process. Sometimes, I had the wrong reasons and the wrong motives, and sometimes even the wrong ideas, but as Romans 8:31 says, "If God is for us, who can be against us?"

I'm convinced that at that time God had a purpose to help me understand how to master money. If I hadn't gone through those experiences, I wouldn't be able to share what I've learned. It wasn't until several years later that I began to understand that mastering my money wasn't so I could go play golf every day. It wasn't about becoming free enough to quit my job. I learned how to master money so I could become free to do God's will and empower others by teaching them how to find this same financial freedom.

I constantly work at mastering money. I always think and pray, *Does God want me to do this or does God not want me to do this?* It's no longer about whether or not I have the money to do it. It's about what I am supposed to do.

One of my greatest blessings has been donating to certain ministries or endeavors. And one of my greatest delights has been helping people overseas by starting nonprofits like Tricord Global and Wealthbuilders. (You can learn more at tricordglobal.com and wealthbuildersinc.org.) Through these organizations, we are able to provide loans and educations to people who really need help.

When you get to the point in your life where you are the master of your money, there is immense freedom. But you have to continuously work on it and resubmit to God's will in your life.

> Then you say in your heart, 'My power and the might of my hand have gained me this wealth.' And you shall remember the Lord your God for it is He who gives you the power to get wealth, that He may establish His covenant which He swore to your fathers, as it is this day.
>
> **Deuteronomy 8:17-18**

I had to go through this process. Even though I was born again, filled with the Holy Spirit, and knew the Word of God, the motives of my heart were not right. I got to a point in my life where I thought, I did this by the work of *my* hand. Look how smart *I* am, and look at everything *I* did. Everybody look at *me* and the wealth *I've* gained. But when you get to that point in your life, you are at a dangerous point. You can't serve God *and* money.

The minute where I said in my heart, "Look it is by *my* hand and *my* might that I gained this wealth," I started serving money again. Even though I was technically free, I was serving money because I measured who I was by what I had.

> **For the love of money is a root of all kinds of evil.**
>
> 1 Timothy 6:10

Let's be crystal clear. You can love money whether you have a dime or not. You can love money whether you're a billionaire or below the poverty line. Unfortunately, I fell in love with money, and even though God is able to work all things for good, I had let Him down. I sinned. He had to do some healing in my life to move money out of my heart. The minute you fall in love with what you have, you begin to keep it from God. The minute you forget that it is God who gave you the power to get wealth, you begin to get off track. And it's at that moment money becomes your master—instead of the other way around.

ESTABLISHING THE COVENANT

Why does God give you the power to get wealth? That He may establish His covenant. Where is He going to establish His covenant? In the earth. The covenant has already been established in heaven. Therefore, we are to be busy establishing the covenant in the earth.

Jesus says, "You cannot serve God and money" (Matthew 6:24). When we establish the covenant in the earth, we are serving God and mastering money. In the next chapter, I want to teach you the steps you can take so that you will be empowered to begin the journey toward mastering money. As you begin to find the money that already has your name on it, the treasures of darkness and the hidden riches of secret places will start coming to you.

It's God or money. You cannot serve both God and money.

Money is just the middle man. In reality, money prevents us from having to carry chickens and bushels of apples with us to buy things. We have this freedom because money acts as the currency in the middle.

The Good Samaritan didn't just have a kind heart. He had the resources to help in the case of an emergency. Wealth is a good thing. It's like this quote: "I was put on earth to get rich, to collect the money that already had my name on it, and then give it all away."

The minute you fall in love with what you have, you will keep it from God. The minute you forget that it is God who gives you the power to get wealth, you will get off track. At that moment, money becomes your master.

"Remember the Lord your God for it is He who gives you the power to get wealth (Deuteronomy 8:18)." Why? That He may establish His covenant. Where is He going to establish His covenant? In the earth. The covenant has already been established in heaven, so we are to be busy establishing the covenant here.

CHAPTER TWO:

GOD'S PURPOSE FOR WEALTH

Then you say in your heart, 'My power and the might of my hand have gained me this wealth.' And you shall remember the Lord your God for it is He who gives you the power to get wealth, that He may establish His covenant which He swore to your fathers, as it is this day.

—Deuteronomy 8:17-18

As Christians, we tend to take a fearful approach to wealth. But as we look back to Deuteronomy 8, we read about how God taught the Jewish people to view wealth. We can learn a lot from their approach. The first five books of the Old Testament are called the Pentateuch or the Torah. The book of Deuteronomy is one of those books, which means that Jews, as well as Christians, believe in this book.

A western mindset can help us understand that the Bible was written from an eastern mindset. We try to translate it, adapt it and apply it in our western culture, but sometimes there are truths that we don't quite understand. That's when it's helpful to think about the cultural background of the Bible. When we look at the book of Deuteronomy or any books of the Torah, it's important to remember that we are reading from a Jewish mindset or perspective. We, therefore, need to understand the origin of the text's individual words.

Jewish Economic Theory was most clearly synthesized for me in an article I read called "Judaism, Markets and Capitalism: Separating Myths from Reality," by Corrine and Robert M. Sauer. In the Jewish Economic Theory, Sauer and Sauer list five foundations:

1. Participation in the creative process

2. Protection of private property

3. The accumulation of wealth as a virtue

4. Caring for the needy

5. Limited government

These five foundations can help us understand what it looks like for God to give us the power to get wealth.

FOUNDATION ONE:
PARTICIPATION IN THE CREATIVE PROCESS

The Jewish people believe that when it comes to wealth, they are able to participate in the creative process with God. In the New Testament, the apostle Paul tells us in 2 Corinthians 6:1 that we are co-laborers together with God. In other words, God has His part to play, and we have our part to play. God's part is grace, while our part is faith. So it's grace and faith, faith and grace, working together in a beautiful cycle.

Here's the best way I know to explain this. I was born and raised in South Texas, home of warmth and humidity. My grandmother used to plant a huge, acre-sized garden every year—which is pretty big to call a garden. I remember this as vividly as if it were yesterday. When I was four or five years old, they plowed the garden with a mule and a wooden plow with a metal blade. A man would stand on the back of the plow and put his weight on the blade, driving the mule to furrow the rows.

Things grow year round in Texas, and by things, I mean weeds! (I'm thankful we're not going to have weeds in heaven.) When the gardening season ended and winter settled in, the plants would die, yet the garden would still fill up with weeds, so my grandmother and her team would go out there with the mule and plow. In a month's time, they cleaned that garden until it was beautiful and green. That was her part in the creative process.

Let's take a look at another illustration.

Together, God had grown a beautiful garden and Dave had tended it.

"Man, God sure created a beautiful garden!" someone exclaimed.

"Yeah," Dave said, "but you should have seen it when God had it all by Himself!"

In other words, we are co-laborers together with God. This foundation in the Jewish Economic Theory means that the Jewish people believe they are active participants with God in the creative process. So as we are here in the earth, we are bringing what Jesus said in Matthew 6 to life: "Thy Kingdom come, thy will be done in the earth…"

When we empower people to participate in the creative process, it's amazing what God can do. I remember a lady in an African village who did four loans with my non-profit, Tricord Global. She took the first loan and started a business for herself. It was just a small stand that provided some dried goods and other items in her village. By the time of the fourth loan, she had a whole grocery store and employed 14 people in her village with full-time work. This lady raised the whole economic standard of that small village. She was also able to put a roof on her house, pay for her kids' schooling, and feed and clothe her family. It was a miracle!

FOUNDATION TWO:
PROTECTION OF PRIVATE PROPERTY

This second foundation says that it's important to have property, or in other words, to become an owner. When you own something, you have the opportunity to become a steward of that which you own.

From the very beginning of the Bible, we see that God gave His people land. He gave Eden to Adam and Eve, and said: "Fill the earth and subdue it." He gave the Promised Land to Abraham and his descendants and said: "Get out of your country...to a land I will show you." Later, in Numbers 13:2, we read, "Send men to spy out the land of Canaan, which I am giving to the children of Israel...".

In many ways, the Old Testament is really the story of God trying to give His people a place to live. He is always looking to give us ownership, whether it be land, businesses, or assets. He loves to give us the opportunity to be stewards.

In the example of the garden, my grandma was tilling, planting, weeding, and caring for that garden because it was her garden. You own things either by virtue of the fact that you actually own the land outright or you are renting the space. Regardless, that space is still your space, and you get to steward it.

At Tricord Global, we provide loans, primarily micro-finance loans, to developing nations. These investments help the people— and thereby the villages, cities, and nations— move forward and begin to transform.

The idea of ownership is not foreign to the western mindset. In some cultures, however, the idea of ownership and protection of private property is not even a possibility. One of the problems we've discovered while working in Africa is that a lot of people don't have a physical address. In these third-world countries, people are often living out in the bushes or in villages, or even in cities, but are unable to actually purchase property.

In many cases, there are no title deeds to property so people don't actually own property in the way that we think of owning property in the West. Now thankfully, that's slowly beginning to change. However, when we look at the protection of private property, we need to realize that in developing nations there is often no such thing as protection of private property because there is no private property. And that's quite a challenge!

FOUNDATION THREE:
THE ACCUMULATION OF WEALTH AS A VIRTUE

The accumulation of wealth as a virtue is the next foundation. In Jewish Economic Theory, the Jews believe that accumulating wealth is a good thing. But in a western mindset, often because of some of our religious training, we tend to think of poverty as a virtue.

I often hear people ask why Jewish people have all the money or why they're always prosperous. The reason is this: They think differently than we do. They see the accumulation of wealth as a virtuous endeavor. In other words, if I am partnering with God and functioning with Money Mastery principles, then as I move forward in life, there is an accumulation process. If I'm thinking properly, managing correctly, and stewarding honestly, I will naturally begin to accumulate wealth.

The Jewish mindset sees being able to steward and manage wealth as being "holy in the earth." However, this is not usually the case in our western mindset. We must remember that it is the Lord our God who gives us the power to get wealth. He is our Master. We are here to serve Him, and in the process of serving God, we will become the master of our money. We do not need to be afraid of building wealth when God is the one empowering us to do so.

FOUNDATION FOUR:
CARING FOR THE NEEDY

The fourth foundation is about caring for the needy with your wealth. Jesus made it clear when He said, "For you have the poor with you always." (Mark 14:7)

When we look at poverty in third-world countries, there is an important distinction we need to make about caring for the needy. If we take Africa—where I've personally had the most experience—there have been many studies done in recent years showing that aid from western nations has created a welfare mentality among the people. The people don't feel the need to till their garden because they can just go to a truck and get a meal. I always like to use this classic example: Instead of giving somebody a fish so they can eat the fish, teach them how to fish. Then they will always have food.

Let me be clear—aid is important when people cannot help themselves. For example, in an emergency crisis like the Ebola outbreak of 2014, or earthquakes and famines, we should definitely be sending aid. Other instances arise in which people need aid because they are sick or experiencing some other type of devastation in which they are unable to help themselves. There have been times with Tricord Global we went in and spent money to drill a water well because the people in the area didn't have the money to do so. In these cases, aid is absolutely important, and we must not neglect to give it.

The reason we give loans is not because we're trying to get the money back. That's not the point. Here's an example of what happens when we offer loans in these countries. Sometimes, philanthropists buy sewing machines for people in developing nations. Then a year later when they go back, they discover that the sewing machines have been dismantled and sold for parts or are sitting around covered in dust because the people weren't trained to use them. In other words, no one ever taught them how to do business.

The reason we give loans is because it brings people back to us every week. When we collect the loan payment, we offer training, teaching, coaching, and mentoring in order to empower them. They walk away from the deal thinking, I paid my loan back. I'm worth something.

I would estimate that as a result of these loans, about 95 percent of those who receive a loan from us completely break into another level of empowerment in their lives. It changes their lives! Additionally, the money that was lent to that person now gets to be lent to another person, therefore perpetuating the cycle of empowerment.

You may ask, "What's the point?" Well, if accumulation of wealth is a virtue, then we as Christians—and as people who master our money—never want to neglect caring for the needy. But we want to do it in the right way.

FOUNDATION FIVE:
LIMITED GOVERNMENT

The last foundation of Jewish Economic Theory is limited government. In other words, we don't want the government intervening in our affairs. The government is here to serve not dominate.

Throughout the Old Testament, we see the Israelites pressing God for more governmental structure. Israel, at its finest, reported straight to God for everything it did. And while God pushed back, trying to let His people know that more government is not always a good thing, they kept asking. They asked for a king even though God told them they didn't need a king. So He delivered. And we can read story after story of how their leaders and kings dominated them.

The reality is that more government means higher taxes, and higher taxes stifle enterprise and business. Most employment in America is provided by small businesses, but most employees have no idea that they're costing their business at least 15 percent more than they're being paid because of matching social security, health insurance, unemployment, etc. Most people don't realize that if you take sales tax and add it to your payroll tax then half of your income is going to taxes.

The average employee in America, who does not own his own business, is basically functioning with half of his or her income going to taxes. He pays a gasoline tax every time he goes to the gas station. He pays a sales tax every time he shops. These taxes add up!

Taxes, in their nature, are a good thing. It's important to pay your portion of the national defense. Taxes that are mutually beneficial to a society are important. However, there can come a point where we are stealing wealth out of people's hands in an over-burdensome way.

This last foundation, limited government, is more about the tax structure than anything. The Jews believe there should be government but it should be limited in order to allow people freedom to live and to engage in enterprise.

TIKKUN OLAM:
PERFECTING THE WORLD

Another thing we find in the Jewish mindset is the consideration of work to be the same as worship. When we study the Old Testament, there are several words in the Hebrew language for the word worship. Avodah is one of the primary words for worship, and it also means "work."

Since the Jews see the accumulation of wealth as a virtue and believe that they're partnering with God in the creative process, they see work as worship.

In Secrets of Jewish Wealth Revealed, Rabbi Celso Cukierkorn writes:

> One of the great differences that set Jews apart from other cultural groups is that we see our wealth as a means to partner with God, as a way to bring God's Kingdom into this earth, a concept that we call *tikkun olam — perfecting the world*. We perfect the world by using our God-given wealth to further God's realm on this planet. So, what you see is that the Jewish people's pursuit of wealth is often paired with the pursuit of charitable works, not only for selfish purposes.

Jesus prayed in Matthew 6:10, "Your kingdom come. Your will be done, on earth, as it is in heaven." We must understand that when we partner with God and live as a blessing to the earth, it's not about becoming this rough, gruff business person. It's about becoming a godly man or woman who is functioning by God's laws of wealth.

When we function by God's laws of wealth and practice His principles, we automatically become a blessing to the world. But we miss it when we think that we are a blessing only when we give. It's true, we are a blessing when we give, tithe, and bring offerings—but we can do so much more!

The problem we sometimes have in the church is that the only place we see true empowerment is in the area of giving. As a result, we give people a fish. We give a lot of fish. Believe me, to support Christian ministries and local churches, we need to bring our tithes and our offerings, but let's be crystal clear. There is an empowerment process that happens with your employees. There is an empowerment process that happens when you bring people up in their lives economically. It is empowering to enable an individual to have their own business or assets. We honor God when we make these things happen through our position in life by bringing a greater expression of God's power, grace, and anointing into people's lives. We are a blessing!

The Jewish mindset allows for these things. They live by this principle. It's not about paying your bills or having more. Sure, there's nothing wrong with being blessed personally, but it's about how we express our blessings.

Rabbi Cukierkorn says it very plainly when he talks about tikkun olam, which means "perfecting the world." Perfecting the world? What are you talking about? Rabbi Cukierkorn also said this:

> "To be religious Jews, we are not supposed to isolate ourselves on a mountaintop and meditate, nor are we to take vows of poverty. Rather, we are supposed to get out into the world, interact with it, and elevate the mundane. This, in fact, is the traditional meaning again of "tikkun olam." We repair the world by elevating it to the holy."

In other words, when we get involved in this wealth-creation process, we are taking the mundane and elevating it to the holy—as long as we're doing it God's way. If the Lord our God gives us the power to get wealth, then it is God who empowers us to have an impact in our world. It's not just about living and waiting until we get out of here. It's about Matthew 6: "Thy Kingdom come, thy will be done in the earth as it is in heaven." This is what it looks like when we partner with God in the earth to take the mundane and elevate it to the holy in order to make His kingdom come.

YOUR KINGDOM COME

In this manner, therefore, pray: our Father in heaven, hallowed be your name, your Kingdom come, your will be done on earth as it is in heaven. Give us this day our daily bread and forgive us our debts as we forgive our debtors and do not lead us into temptation, but deliver us from the evil one. For yours is the Kingdom and the power and the glory forever. Amen.

—The Lord's Prayer, Matthew 6:9-13

We can have an impact in cities and nations when we understand tikkun olam. Our partnership with God in this creative process will transform them—one person at a time.

Years ago in Africa, an evangelist preached to a crowd of almost a million people. Some 300,000 people came to Jesus in that crusade. Followers of a different religion, however, had another strategy. Instead of holding a crusade, they came in after the crusade and targeted the families who attended. They went in and offered the families small micro-finance loans and said, "If you convert, we'll give you this loan." Sadly, many people turned and walked away from Jesus. They took the loans.

As Christians in America, we often only understand the gospel of salvation and forget about the gospel of the kingdom. But in the New Testament, Jesus came preaching the gospel of the kingdom of heaven. Paul also taught on the kingdom of God. Now I am by no means downplaying the vital nature of the gospel of salvation. You must be born again. Jesus said, "I'm the way, the truth, and the life. No one comes to the Father except through Me." (John 14:6)

That is exactly how a person comes into the Kingdom of God—by being born again. That's how we come into a relationship with God. So the problem doesn't lie with our focus on the gospel of salvation. The problem is that we forget to preach the gospel of the Kingdom. We forget about tikkun olam.

I've seen alcoholics and drug addicts get delivered from their addictions and become born again. As they begin to feed on the Word of God, their lives are changed. But they need to have some-where to advance into on this earth. They need to learn financial management tools, job skills and relational abilities. I'm convinced the whole thing is about both the gospel of salvation and the gospel of the Kingdom.

> **And Jesus came and spoke to them, saying, 'All authority has been given to Me in heaven and on earth. Go there-fore and make disciples of all the nations, baptizing them in the name of the Father and of the Son and of the Holy Spirit, teaching them to observe all things that I have**

commanded you; and lo, I am with you always, even to the end of the age.' Amen.

Matthew 28:19

I believe that Jesus is saying that we are called to disciple all those in the nations, as well as the nations themselves! City and nation transformation can't take place without a kingdom economy. It starts with transforming the lives of individuals who make up those cities and nations.

If they're in a place long enough, the Jewish people can take over a nation. They can do this because of how they think about wealth and the kingdom. They have a kingdom mindset. Oral Roberts once said, "Whoever controls the finances of a city or nation will control the spiritual climate as well." So as Christians, we must expand our thinking and understand that kingdom economic empowerment is essential for us to see cities and nations transformed.

There is a marketplace sound, or wind, that is blowing in the earth and in the church. God is doing something right now in our world. He is speaking to the hearts of His people about entering the marketplace as a force for the kingdom. And people are responding. They may express it in different ways, but the sound is being heard.

In 2015, I spoke at a business summit for Charis Bible College in Colorado. Five hundred Christian business people attended those meetings! That kind of attendance showed us that the church is ready to start getting into the marketplace.

This marketplace sound led me to start an organization called Wealthbuilders. In Wealthbuilders , we empower people all over the world by educating them in business so that they can rise out of poverty. The importance of people learning to take scriptural business principles and apply them in the earth cannot be underestimated.

In August 2014, I held a Wealthbuilders Conference in Ethiopia. After the conference, I received this email:

> Thank you so much for the progress and determination in doing the seminar here in Ethiopia. As all of you may remember, I have tried to highlight some points to be considered into your teachings, which you have in mind.

> To sum up, it is urgent for the church to be aware and involved in this business world where everyone's language is about business. If you stay for a few days in Ethiopia and listen, people are passionate to be business owners, grow economically… and in the midst of movement, I think the church is not sure of the way she can be involved. Largely, the church is not sure of the way she can be involved in. Members including most leaders do not have clear insight in this regard. Ordained church ministers are worrying how to do it besides their ministry. There are so many issues and challenges relating to this timely issue. In developing nations like Ethiopia, sound teaching in this regard is like laying the foundation to redeem the generation to come.

This man is over 5,000 churches in Ethiopia. He defined this marketplace sound as a movement. When I spoke at this conference in Ethiopia, the whole crowd came alive. There was a buzz, because in the hearts and minds of people wherever we go in the world there is an understanding of a marketplace, kingdom sound in the earth. God has bigger plans and bigger purposes. He wants to see His people empowered so that we can see His Kingdom come on earth as it is in heaven.

SEVEN MOUNTAINS

One of the ways we can bring God's Kingdom to earth is by making sure that we, as Christians, are active in all areas of our culture. I personally like to use the Seven Mountains to explain this. The Seven Mountains were imagined by Bill Bright and Loren Cunningham. It is a concept that is not necessarily found in scripture, yet it helps us understand something really amazing. The Seven Mountains are what we would call the mountains of society or culture.

On the earth, as people come together in a city or nation, there are seven primary categories that people tend to fall into: business, arts/entertainment, media, government, education, family, or religion.

CHURCH

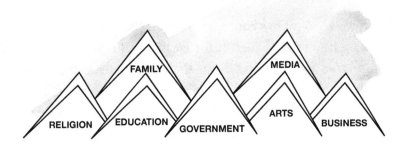

I use the term "Religion Mountain" on purpose because the church itself is not religion. Above all of these mountains, I wrote the word, "Church," because it's God's plan that the church of Jesus Christ be involved in every mountain. We're starting to see this happen in America in Christian companies like Chick-fil-A, where God is honoring and blessing at the highest level. We also see strong Christians in government. We're even starting to see some godly films come out of Hollywood because Christians are getting involved in the "Arts Mountain."

All of these mountains are being affected by Christians, and that's how it should be. Young people, who come to faith, often have no idea how they can impact the world for God. The only thing they know to do is go to Bible College. They have no idea that they can work for the Lord in these other six mountains. Of course, I believe in going to Bible College. In fact, I did it! But the problem is, if all the Christians are only working in the Religion Mountain, then we've got a lot of areas in this world untouched by Christians!

The church is called to be in every mountain. Our young people are called to be in every mountain. When Christians infiltrate all the mountains of society and take their proper place according to the gifts God has given them, we will begin to impact society as a whole. We will then see nations being discipled. In fact, we will see the kingdom of God come to earth—as it is in heaven.

The Seven Mountains concept was not created by business people concerned with building wealth for wealth's sake. It was developed by missionaries who realized from their experiences that believers need to be in other areas of culture—not just religion. Instead of asking people to come to church all of the time, we can surround everyone, and every place, with the church.

Let me preface by saying this: "I don't know the time or the day of Jesus' return. I have no idea." So what am I going to do? I'm going to be urgent. I'm going to be diligent. I'm going to be a kingdom bearer until He comes, and I'm going to go into the mountain that God has called me to infiltrate.

Another reason that we use the idea of mountains is because in Daniel 6:3, we read that Daniel had a more excellent spirit about him. That word "excellent" comes from the Hebrew word *yateer*, which means "to come to a point" or "to rise to the top." Like Daniel, we should rise to the top of whatever mountain God has called us.

> **Now to Him who is able to [carry out His purpose and] do superabundantly more than all that we dare ask or think [infinitely beyond our greatest prayers, hopes, or dreams], according to His power that is at work within us.**
>
> Ephesians 3:20 (AMP)

God works in us all this energy and power by the Holy Spirit that's in us. He does that to carry out His purpose in our lives. So regardless of the mountain you're in, God wants to carry out His purpose for your life in that area.

The problem is that we tend to resist working in the mountain God's called us to. Or like in my own history, I went to the right mountain but for all the wrong reasons. I jumped into the business mountain, in the beginning, for my selfish gain. And because of that, it was tempting to think, Well, God never wants me to go back. But that's not necessarily true. The truth is, maybe God wants you to go back into that area of culture and do what you learned to do, but this time, do it God's way. I always try not to tell God my plans and then ask Him to bless them. Instead, I try to ask, "God, what is Your plan?" because God's plan for my life is already blessed!

MAKING A DIFFERENCE

God's purpose for wealth is to make a difference. For example, take the story of the good Samaritan. Margaret Thatcher said, "Nobody would remember the Good Samaritan if he only had good intentions. He had money as well."

> A Jewish man was traveling from Jerusalem down to Jericho, and he was attacked by bandits. They stripped him of his clothes, beat him up, and left him half dead beside the road. By chance a priest came along. But when he saw the man lying there, he crossed to the other side of the road and passed him by. A Temple assistant walked over and looked at him lying there, but he also passed by on the other side. Then a despised Samaritan came along, and when he saw the man, he felt compassion for him. Going over to him, the Samaritan soothed his wounds with olive oil and wine and bandaged them. Then he put the man on his own donkey and took him to an inn, where he took care of him. The next day he handed the innkeeper two silver coins, telling him, 'Take care of this man. If his bill runs higher than this, I'll pay you the next time I'm here."

> Luke 10:30-35 (NLT)

Many of us, if we're not careful, find that we fall into the same category as the Jewish priest or the Jewish temple assistant. There are two dimensions to this—the "Religion Mountain" and resources.

Sometimes we're so involved in the "Religion Mountain" that we have no ability to relate to people outside of that mountain. The Jewish priest probably had the resources to help the man because of the Jewish belief about wealth as a virtue. Yet he was so engrossed in his "Religion Mountain" that he couldn't break out of it to help him. Now I don't know for sure, but it could be that the Jewish temple assistant didn't have any money to even consider helping the man. But this doesn't excuse him for not even stopping to check on him. Notice that one was too lost in the "Religion Mountain" and one had no ability to help.

The Samaritans were despised by the Jews and weren't accepted or popular by any stretch of the imagination. But evidently, the

Good Samaritan did not allow what the Jews thought about him, or Samaritans in general, to stop him from becoming a prosperous, blessed man who operated in the covenant of God. He didn't let their snootiness and their opinion of him and his people get to him. He refused to accept it. He had resources and could act in the mountain God put him.

He said, "Here's enough money to take care of what the bill should be. And by the way, if it's higher than that, when I come back through, I'll take care of it." Because he was coming back through, and therefore probably traveled a lot, chances are he was some sort of merchant. Because of the mountain God had put him in, he had the finances to bring tikkun olam into that man's life. In other words, he had the resources to take a tragic situation and elevate it into something better.

The Jewish priest and the temple assistant didn't do anything. But then came a despised Samaritan who had resources, understanding and knowhow. And most importantly, he had a heart willing to give sacrificially.

Beloved, I pray that you may prosper in all things.

3 John 2

We need to understand that God wants us to prosper. The primary reason He wants us to prosper is so that we can make Matthew 6:10 come alive: "Your Kingdom come. Your will be done on earth as it is in heaven." He wants us to prosper so that we can partner with Him in the earth by working in all of the mountains.

A friend of mine who is one of the primary teachers on the Seven Mountains in the U.S. told me, "Billy, what people don't understand is that the 'Business Mountain' really is the key to the other six mountains."

I said, "Why do you say that?"

"The reason I say that is because in every mountain, business is involved. Finance and money are involved."

> Then he spoke a parable to them saying, "The ground of a certain rich man yielded plentifully. And he thought within himself, saying, 'What shall I do, since I have no room to store my crops?' So he said, 'I will do this: I will pull down my barns and build greater, and there I will store all my crops and my goods. And I will say to my soul, "Soul, you have many goods laid up for many years; take your ease; eat, drink, and be merry."' But God said to him, 'Fool! This night your soul will be required of you; then whose will those things be which you have provided?' So is he who lays up treasure for himself, and is not rich toward God."
>
> Luke 12:16-21

God wants you to have barns so you can have an impact in the earth. He wants you to have barns so that you can partner with Him in the earth and all of the mountains of society and culture—for the kingdom's cause. The reason God wants you to have barns is not so you can eat, drink, and be merry. God wants you to have barns so that you can make a difference.

I named my nonprofit Wealthbuilders after Deuteronomy 8:18, where we read that God gives us the power and the right to get, build, and grow wealth. In Wealthbuilders, we are: Making sense of making money for making a difference (Wealthbuilders Vision Statement). We're not about trying to build something and heap riches on ourselves.

I want to be clear though. God does want you to be blessed. He wants you to build wealth. He wants you to have some barns. But it's not about building bigger barns. It's about prospering in the barns you already have. When it comes time to build bigger barns, that's where we begin to partner with God in this process of tikkun olam, to bring the mundane up to the holy. That's God's purpose for wealth.

 **SUMMARY**

As Christians, we tend to take a fearful approach to wealth. But as we look to Deuteronomy 8, we read how God taught the Jewish people to view wealth. We can learn a lot from their approach.

Foundation One: Participation in the Creative Process. In the New Testament, the apostle Paul tells us in 2 Corinthians 6:1 that we are co-laborers together with God. In other words, God has His part to play, and we have our part to play. God's part is grace, while our part is faith.

Foundation Two: Protection of Private Property. This second foundation says that it's important to have property or, in other words, to become an owner. When you own something, you have the opportunity to become a steward of that which you own.

Foundation Three: The Accumulation of Wealth as a Virtue. In Jewish Economic Theory, they believe that accumulating wealth is a good thing. The Jewish mindset sees being able to steward and manage wealth as being "holy in the earth." But in our western mindset, most of us don't see it this way.

Foundation Four: Caring for the Needy. Always give aid in times of crisis. But when it comes to general charity, think of the cliché: Instead of giving somebody a fish so they can eat the fish, teach them how to fish. This way, they will always have food.

Foundation Five: Limited Government. This last foundation is more about the tax structure than anything. The Jews believe there should be government, but it should be limited to allow people freedom to live and to engage in enterprise.

Another thing we find in the Jewish mindset is that they consider work to be the same as worship.

There is an understanding of a marketplace, kingdom sound in the earth. God has bigger plans and bigger purposes. He wants to see His people empowered so that we can see His kingdom come on earth as it is in heaven.

Whatever mountain you're in, God wants to carry out His purpose for your life in that area. The church is called to be in every mountain.

God does want you to be blessed. He wants you to build wealth. But it's not about building bigger barns. It's about prospering in the barns you already have. But when it comes time to build bigger barns, that's when we begin to partner with God in this process of tikkun olam, to bring the mundane up to the holy. That's God's purpose for wealth.

CHAPTER THREE:

THE TRIPLE X FACTOR

Over the years, I've developed a finance theory that helps people get from the point of being mastered by money to the point of mastering money. I believe God gave me this tool. I call it the Triple X Factor. And it is the foundation of this book.

There are three levels within the Triple X Factor—First X, Second X and Third X. First X Income is the starting point. First X Income is when you work and get paid for that work. Second X Income is a place of great freedom because this is where you have and manage assets that pay you. Third X is a place of philanthropy. At the Third X, you're giving the majority of your income away.

It's time that we in the body of Christ begin to wake up. Sometimes the church is like a sleeping giant because we haven't been as wise as we should have been when it comes to financial matters. And because of that, we're unable to impact our city or our nation. It's time we as the church learn how to handle our finances and build wealth.

The sad thing is that many of us have been told that God wants to bless us, but we haven't been told how to walk in that blessing. Deuteronomy 8:18 says that it is God who gives us the power to get wealth. The Triple X Factor is a 30,000-foot view of how that can happen in your life. I struggled for a long time, trying to find a way to understand wealth building from a 30,000-foot view.

Whenever I would hear different teachings on wealth building, it felt like I was standing too close to an elephant. For instance, if a man did not know what an elephant was, and someone asked him the question, "What is an elephant," and he only saw the trunk of the elephant, he might say, "Oh, an elephant is a hose." Or, perhaps, if he looked up and only saw the side of the elephant, he might say, "Oh, an elephant is a wall." Maybe he only saw the tail, and said, "An elephant is a rope."

He associated the whole object with only one part. But the truth is, an elephant is more than a trunk, a side, or a tail. An elephant is all of those things. For a long time, I struggled to fit all of the different lessons on wealth building into one solid idea of wealth building. I was looking for wealth building's simple terms.

If I learned something that was a debt-freedom thing, I'd put it over in the debt-freedom compartment in my brain. But I knew that building wealth was more than eliminating debt. I knew the trunk was attached to an elephant, so what I was really dealing with was an elephant. Finally, after many years of experience, discussion, learning and petitioning God, I received The Triple X Factor. This gave me the true 30,000-foot view of wealth building. I finally saw the whole elephant.

THREE KINDS OF MONEY

The First X

With First X income, you work and then you get paid. You put in your time and value, and you get paid for that time and value. Most people are at this First X. First X income is used for tithes, offerings, asset-building, and living. It's also known as "non-leverage income" because of the direct correlation between your time and your paycheck. People in the First X category are usually employees, but some can be self-employed.

Personally, when I receive honorariums for speaking, I'm receiving non-leveraged income. I speak, and I get paid. But I receive leveraged income when I speak and sell product at the back of the room. Most of the time I can make a lot more selling product than I can speaking. I have leveraged myself, because now people get to read, hear and watch what I have to say without me having to be present.

The Second X

Second X income is what we call asset income. You also pay your tithes and offerings out of this. But the point of the Second X is to reach the point where you are completely living off of the income from your assets. It's called foundational wealth, and you also use it to continue to build more assets.

People at the Second X are usually business owners or investors. At the Second X, you still have to work, but instead of working as an employee, the type of work you do is asset management. You manage your assets in order to live. At the Second X, you can take or leave your First X income. Some people choose to keep their jobs, while others choose to march into full-time asset management.

The Third X

The Third X goes beyond the First and Second X. The amount at this income level is excessive; it's beyond what you need. The purpose of Third X Income is for it to be given completely away. You now have more coming in than going out, and you are free to give this income all away. Instead of buying two more houses, or four more Ferraris, you can choose to invest in impacting the world for the kingdom.

At the Third X, you have multiple assets, and you are thinking about preserving and growing wealth. But if you join with God on this wealth adventure, the big picture is seeing people, cities, and nations transformed. You can start pouring it into the Third World and developing nations through microfinance and other means. People's lives can be transformed through you!

You can position yourself to get to this Third X, and whether or not you end up investing or just giving it all away or a combination of both, the point is that you are no longer just interested in a financial return on your money. At the Third X, you have the opportunity to be interested in a social and spiritual return.

The time and talent you trade in First X is work, and then you get paid a certain amount. But the time and talent that you trade in Second X is that you manage your assets, and then you get paid significantly more. In other words, with First X income, you invest one time, and you get paid one time. But in Second X income, you invest one time, and you may get paid ten times. This is because when you create and/or acquire assets and invest and manage those assets, the growth can be exponential if all goes well. Wealth, therefore, is not built at the First X; it's built at the Second X.

In our society, the only time that one-for-one ratio changes is if someone has an extremely high-paying career. Take movie stars, for instance, like Harrison Ford or Sandra Bullock. They do one movie and might get paid $20 million for that one movie. They invest time, the same amount of time you would working, but get paid a whole lot more for that work, right? If we could all be movie stars and musicians, that'd be one thing. But for most people, we invest once and get paid once. That's why it's important to learn how to build Second X income.

TRIPLE X FACTOR

To begin wealth building, you must first find out where you are financially. A safe guess at the average American household income is about $50,000. For some states it's higher and for some lower, but this is a good starting point for our illustration.

When you look at the indebtedness of a typical household in the U.S., you will see more money going out every month than is coming in. If $50,000 represents the average annual income in the U.S., then $54,000 represents the average annual household expenses. And so we are left with one question: How can someone spend more per year than they're actually making?

Unique to western nations is the phenomenon of consumer credit. We can easily buy things that immediately depreciate in value by using our consumer credit. We can buy things like TV's and clothes on credit because we have credit cards or other types of installment accounts. Therefore, in America, it's exceptionally easy to spend more than you make.

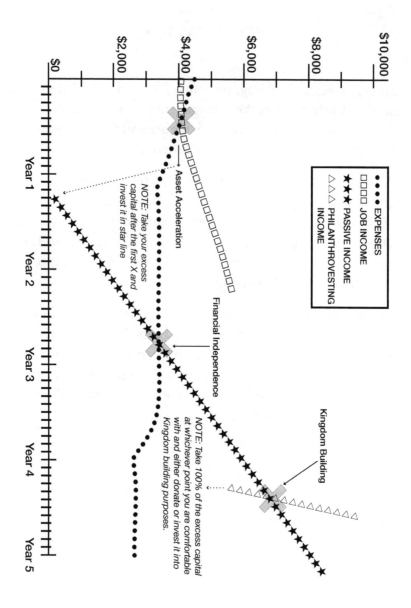

On the Triple X chart, the left axis represents monthly income. Notice that we have $2,000, $4,000, $6,000, $8,000 and $10,000 marked. These marks represent income per month. The bottom axis represents time in months, marked with years one through five.

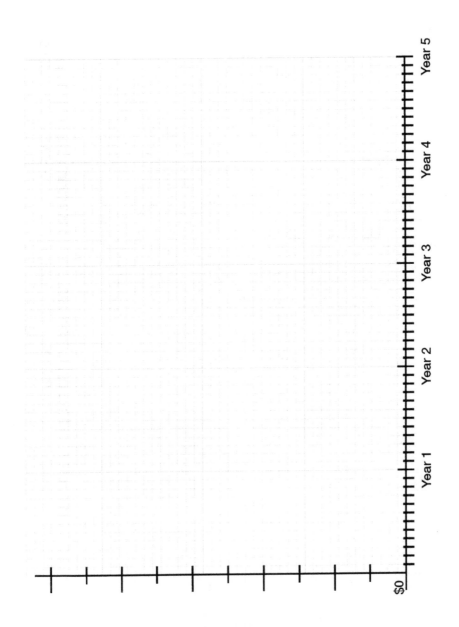

SAMPLE WORKSHEET PAGE

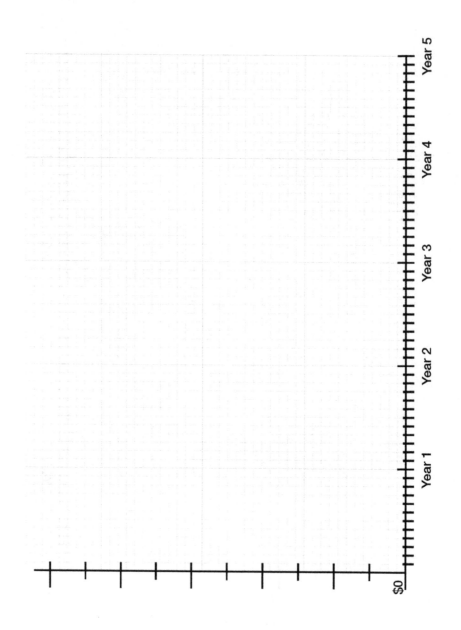

SAMPLE WORKSHEET PAGE

Each dot represents one month of expenses. So for this illustration, at the beginning, we have about $4,500 going out each month.

It's important to position yourself in order to build wealth. I recommend building your own personal chart based off of this.

1. Plot your expenses each month.

To fill out your own chart, you need to be very honest about your expenses. Start with the month you're in right now. Begin to chart your monthly expenses. For instance, let's say you start in April, and the total outgo of expenses in March was $2,500. You would place an asterisk at the $2,500 mark. Then at the end of April, you would place an asterisk representing how much you spent in April.

Once you start implementing the tools in this book, you should begin to see your expenses go down. This will allow you to start paying off your debt while learning how to handle your finances better. However, for a lot of people, expenses don't come down. They remain the same or may even go up until they can get control of their spending. If this happens to you, that's okay. Start where you are, and with time, prayer, and work, you will eventually learn how to master this expense line.

2. Plot your income each month.

Each square in the line represents monthly income. Chart your first month's income in the same way that you charted your first monthly expenses. This line will probably stay horizontal for a while. But again, after you implement what you learn in this book, you'll be able to start bringing value to the marketplace. And when you start bringing value to the marketplace, your income will begin to go up.

3. Build your First X.

Now for some people, the First X is in good shape. In other words, they have more income than expenses. If this is the case, they can start building the Second X. But for most people, the First X is going to be in rougher shape. This means that they have more expenses than income. In this instance, the squares representing monthly income will stay even for now, but the dots—monthly expenses—are going to come down.

Most people will be able to start controlling their expenses, especially their consumer debt, before they start increasing their income. That's completely normal. Start working on your expenses immediately by cutting things out, making extra, or driving down debt. It will take a little longer to grow your income.

When it comes to your income, always remember this: You take value to the marketplace not time. Most people think they take time because they get paid per hour, but the truth is money is attracted not pursued. So when you start working on yourself harder than you do on your job, you will get paid more for your job. This is because you become more valuable.

As your expenses begin to come down and your income begins to go up, you start to form the First X. In other words, you are in a position to begin building wealth. The First X is a great place to be. You either get out of debt, or gain control of it, and start mastering your finances. There is some teaching available out there on this aspect, but there's not a lot on how to reach the Second X.

4. Gain assets.

Keep graphing your income and expense lines every month so you can monitor exactly where you are. For example, as the First X forms, you'll notice a gap developing between the line of squares and the dots. That gap is the excess capital that you now have available to you. What you do with that excess capital determines whether or not you will build wealth. You might be tempted to just spend it all, thereby not building any wealth. Now, the good news is that at least you're not getting into more consumer debt by doing this (hopefully). But the bad news is that you are still not building wealth.

The real key to building wealth is learning to invest your excess capital. Put that excess capital to work so you can begin to gain assets that produce income in your life. Start using this gap to create Second X income. For some people, it may take two, three, or even four years to reach a point where they have any excess capital to deploy or invest. That's okay. Stay with it, and you'll get there!

In this particular example, we're looking at a 12-month period. Pay attention to the first asterisk on the left. That asterisk represents your first investment. You're probably not going to have enough money to put a down payment on a piece of real estate, but you will have enough to open a savings account.

A while back, I was teaching at a conference at the Omni Hotel in Dallas, Texas. When I finished teaching on real estate, two huge guys, about 6'5", came up to me. They said, "We're ready to invest in real estate!"

They were pumped up from the talk, so I looked at them and said, "Well, do you have any money?"

"Well, no, we don't have any money. But we're excited and ready to invest."

So here's what I said: "When you have $10,000 through whatever means, in your possession, call me. I'll fly to Dallas at my expense, and I'll teach you how to buy your first investment property."

Six months later, one of the guys called me. He had $10,000, so I flew to Texas and helped him get started. Today he owns more than 60 individual properties—multi-family units and single-family houses.

You might ask, "What does this have to do with the first asterisk?" Well, here's what he did. He went home and immediately started saving. He had a good income and put some money into a savings account. That was his first asterisk. By doing this, he put himself in a position to begin acquiring assets. The goal is that the asterisks, representing income from assets, will progress upward and form a line.

Of course, if you put your money in a savings account, your return will be very low. That's not a lot of income. But if you, instead, put your money into assets with a better return, the asterisks will really start to accelerate.

A simple illustration of an asset that brings income is rental properties (single-family) with positive cash flow. The more of this type of investments that you can accumulate, the more the snowball will start rolling in the right direction.

The good news is that as you build wealth, all of a sudden your cars and mortgage will be paid off. The beauty of this is that when your house and cars are paid off, it doesn't cost a lot to live, and the dots, your expenses, will continue to come down.

Note: You can start the asterisks without ever accomplishing the First X. If you're not in a financial position to acquire assets, you can create assets instead and start the asterisks early. An example of creating an asset is starting a business like an eBay or Etsy shop, outside of your day job, that has immediate cash flow. Then you can use that cash flow from the business to start investing in assets or paying off debt.

Another way to do this would be to borrow for the purpose of investing in assets. I know many people who have started investing in real estate by taking out a second mortgage on their personal home. If they have enough real estate knowledge and acquire assets slowly (at least in the beginning), they can build Second X income from that acquired real estate.

5. Build the Second X.

The key to the Triple X Factor is when the asterisks begin to take off as you acquire excess capital and put it into things that produce income for you. You will start investing and receiving better and better returns. Here's what happens once this occurs:

The dots will continue to go down, and all of a sudden, the asterisks will cross the dots. This means that your cost of living is covered by passive income! The moment that the asterisks become more than your cost of living is the moment you become financially free. That's the moment when, if you want, you can quit your job.

Because of God's grace and help, I was able to reach financial independence in my personal life in two and a half years. But for some people, it may take a lot longer than that. It could take some people ten years to do this.

A lot of people ask me what their first goal should be when starting to build wealth, and I always tell them what the Triple X Factor says: Your first goal—your first big goal—should be to replace your earned income with passive income. That's it! That's the key to start experiencing financial independence.

Most of the time, the financial industry in America tells you to put your asterisk money in a 401k, an IRA, or some other type of retirement account. It's definitely wise to have a retirement account set up—but that is a slow process. It can take a long time to build up wealth that way!

Many people—who retire with a decent portfolio—have never taken the time to learn how to invest, because they never understood how taxes could steal their wealth. When they retire, they end up paying more taxes in what we call "tax-deferred accounts" than they were paying when they were actually working and making a salary. The minute they start pulling that money out of those normal IRA's and 401k's, they have to pay earned-income tax on that money. After all is said and done, they end up having much less than they thought they had.

The good news is that we have another instrument called the Roth IRA. Young people should certainly take advantage of this tool, because that money grows tax free down the road. Then when you pull the money out, you don't have to pay earned-income tax on it. The best news, however, is that when you reach this point of financial independence, you can continue to grow an amazing portfolio, invest in all kinds of things, and truly begin to build wealth.

6. Build the Third X.

Remember on the First X when the dotted line crossed the line of squares and we had a gap? The same thing happens here. When the asterisks cross the dotted line, we will have another gap that represents excess capital again. It's at that point that I marked: "Quit job."

You may ask, "Well, what do you do with that new excess capital?" This is the moment you can choose to really partner with God in building wealth. If you're being blessed, you will come to a point, as in the story in Luke, where you have a big choice. You can choose to build bigger barns, eat, drink and be merry. But Jesus called this option foolish. Why? Because the Jewish mindset sees wealth accumulation as a virtue. But it's not for the purpose of building bigger barns.

This is where the Third X comes in. Somewhere in that excess capital gap, you will reach a point where you can start giving all of your income away, and invest some of your assets for a social and spiritual impact. At this point, you don't just give away ten percent for tithe. Now everything you earn—100% from this passive income

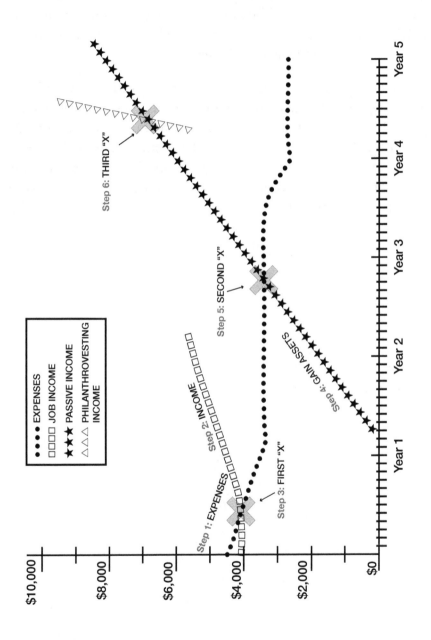

above the point where the asterisks meets the triangles—can be given away! You have reached the place where you and your family are already taken care of. You've got a nice barn; you're financially independent; you could even quit your job if you chose to. You're completely and totally financially free!

You can now choose to direct all of that excess money to kingdom purposes. You may think, How does this actually work? Well, you still pay your tithes and offerings at the First X and Second X, but in the Third X, you are now in the position to give all of your money away in order to see the kingdom of God established in the earth. "Thy Kingdom come, thy will be done, in earth, as it is in heaven" (Matthew 6:10).

 **SUMMARY**

Over the years, I've developed a finance theory that helps people get from the point of being mastered by money to the point of mastering it. I really believe God gave me this tool, and I call it the "Triple X Factor." The Triple X Factor is the foundation of this book.

With First X income, you work and then you get paid. You put in your time and value, and you get paid for that time and value. Most people are at this First X.

Second X income is what we call asset income. People at the Second X are usually business owners or investors.

The Third X goes beyond all of this. The amount at this income level is excessive. It's beyond what you need. The purpose of Third X income is to be given completely away.

CHAPTER FOUR:

SEVEN STEPS TO FINANCIAL FREEDOM

STEP 1:
ESCALATE

The first step to financial freedom is to escalate by increasing your ability to earn. I had the opportunity to share this advice with several government ministers in Uganda when they came to a Triple X Factor presentation in Kampala. In that gathering of leaders (about 25 people), I was fascinated by some of the questions they asked. As we went around the room discussing the Triple X Factor, one of the younger men in the group asked, "What do we do here in Kampala when we don't have a lot of resources or capital to be able to start businesses? What do we do?"

I told him that the one thing that he could do that wouldn't cost him a lot of money was to increase his knowledge about how to do business and how to make money. I told him to seek education in any form. There are all kinds of people, myself included, who are giving free content out to the world on how to do business and build wealth. Take advantage of this! Read blogs and books. Listen to podcasts and watch videos. Find mentors in the area of wealth building.

You increase your ability to earn by increasing your knowledge, understanding, and wisdom because you get paid for value—not for time. The more you know and have on your resumé, the more you can earn. In other words: the more you learn, the more you earn.

STEP 2:
ELIMINATE

The second step to financial freedom is to eliminate consumer debt. Consumer debt is an impasse in our ability to increase our wealth. When you have debt, you pay interest, and that interest takes away from the money that you could be using to build wealth. In other words, you're actually building someone else's wealth when you pay interest. That's why it's very important to eliminate consumer debt.

In the First X, the squares are going up because you're escalating your ability to earn. And the dots are going down because you're eliminating consumer debt. This illustrates first two steps to reaching the First X—escalate your ability to earn, and eliminate consumer debt.

You might ask, "Will this cause me to build wealth?" Of course not! You won't build wealth by just eliminating consumer debt, but these two steps will put you in a position to start building wealth.

The amount of consumer debt in America is insane. The total outstanding U.S. revolving debt (including credit card debt but not mortgage debt) in 2013 was $847 billion. That's just in the U.S.! Our debt is equal to the gross domestic product of Belgium and

Denmark—combined! Yet we wonder in the U.S. why we can't get ahead.

In the next chapter, I'll walk you through how to eliminate consumer debt.

STEP 3:
ACCUMULATE

Now it's time to move forward to the third step to financial freedom: accumulate. Accumulating wealth is the beginning of the Second X. At this step, you will save for emergencies and start saving for a home. First, create a savings account and stock it up for several months, and then start saving for a home (that is, if you don't already have one).

In the First X you will learn to live on 80 percent of your income. You will have 10 percent going to your tithes and another 10 percent going to your investments. If you are able, and really want to escalate your wealth, you can live off of 70 percent of your income. Here's what this would look like: you would tithe 10 percent, professionally invest 10 percent, and personally invest 10 percent.

Regardless of whether you're living off of 70 percent or 80 percent of your income at this step, one of the first things you should do is take 10 percent and put it toward an emergency savings account. I suggest setting aside three to six months of your living expenses toward this account. Of course, not everyone will opt to have this emergency fund, but I strongly encourage you to have some source of cash besides your credit cards to operate with in case the need arises.

Once you've completed this emergency fund, you can start using that same 10 percent to save up for a home. A lot of people ask about renting and buying. As long as you are settling down in an area for a while and are able to not overpay for a property, I would suggest that you buy instead of rent. Remember when you buy your first house, you're buying an asset. Therefore, it will appreciate in value.

Today with the FHA, a government mortgage program, you can buy a home for 3 percent down (if there is another Great Recession, this rate will change). There are also some programs for brand new home buyers that will actually give you the down payment. At this step, it's important for you to start saving for a home. Remember, you're positioning yourself to build wealth.

STEP 4:
PARTICIPATE

Now that you've actively saved for a home, it's time for the fourth step: participate. You participate by purchasing your home and opening a Roth IRA. You need to purchase your own home before you start buying investment property. Owning an asset, and managing it closely, will really grow you before you move on to build the Second X.

There are certain advantages to purchasing your own home. One advantage is that you will have a capital gains exemption. This means that if the home is your primary residence, you can make up to $500,000 profit on your house, tax-free. Not tax deferred, tax free! This is a wonderful thing.

For young people especially, I encourage you to open a Roth IRA. We'll talk about different types of IRA's later but the simple principle is this: Each year that you put money into a Roth IRA, you don't get to take that money as a tax deduction for that year. However, all of the earnings in that Roth IRA, over that whole period of time, are tax free. Plus, you can borrow against that IRA on the money you put in (not including the earnings). You can borrow on it with no penalty or issue. For instance, you might use it for a down payment on a house. A Roth IRA is almost always the best way to go as far as IRA's are concerned. In order to participate, you must purchase a home and start building a Roth IRA.

After I had gone through this process of participation (buying a home), I really accelerated. The most real estate transactions I've ever done in one year was about 200. But before I could accelerate, I had to participate. So I bought a home and then borrowed against the equity in my home to start investing in real estate. Then when I really got big. I actually closed my IRA, took the penalty hit, which was quite substantial, and used that cash to invest in my real estate business.

Here's the point: You have to start building some kind of asset base, and the simplest way to do this, based on the tax laws in the U.S., is to open a Roth IRA and buy your own home. If you get those two things started, you will have a solid asset base. This is how you begin to build the asterisks to get to the Second X.

STEP 5:
ACCELERATE

The fifth step to financial freedom is: accelerate. There are three primary ways to accelerate: invest in real estate, invest in the stock market, and invest in your own business.

Invest in real estate: You should learn to invest in real estate in addition to your personal home. Most people who have higher levels of wealth have invested in real estate. It doesn't necessarily mean that they are receiving income from their real estate, but it does mean that they are holding their wealth in real estate.

For example, when you hear about the ten homes that Oprah Winfrey or someone has around the world, you should understand why they have them. Most of the time, it's not because they are some rich person trying to show off all of their wealth. One of the primary reasons they own multiple homes (real estate) is for tax planning.

Here's how this works: They will set up a real estate business because they're kicking off so much cash from their business. Then they roll that cash over into real estate because that will typically hold its value in comparison to other investments. Then they will use the write-offs on the depreciation of that property to shelter the income they're making. This is brilliant, wealth-building tax planning!

When you're building to the Second X, you need to invest in real estate to get income that will help you attain financial independence. That's not your only option for building wealth, though. Let's take a look at the second option: invest in the stock market. This is my least favorite of the three ways to accelerate your wealth. The most important thing to learn about investing in the stock market is how to position yourself so you don't lose money.

Warren Buffett, the sage of Omaha, said the secret to making money is not losing money. Personally, I have lost a lot of money in the stock market, but the good news is that I had the money to lose. And the better news is that, overall, I still made more than I lost. When I started out, I lost a lot of money when I acted before having knowledge, understanding, and wisdom in the right areas.

The third way to accelerate your wealth is to: invest in your own business. You can invest in real estate, as well as the stock market, without first building your own business. You can still have First X income and take the excess that's coming off of that and invest it in real estate and/or the stock market. When you properly build a business, that business will actually replace the income from the First X.

Some people are able to still do both. For instance, let's look at Peyton Manning. He gets paid as a quarterback for the Denver Broncos. That's his First X income (and it's a lot more than most of us will ever make with First X). He gets a big contract and makes a lot of money, but in addition to this he also does commercials for Papa John's and Best Buy. (He also purchased a couple of Papa John's.) These things have nothing to do with actually playing football; they have to do with what he is. He actually set up a business to receive income from advertising.

You can go straight from the First X to the Second X and build a business this way, but the key is that you have to know what you're doing. You have to have some sort of consistent income in your life. Most of the time, it takes even the most successful businesses about three years to become profitable. Sometimes it takes a little longer to actually live out of the income like you need to on the Second X.

I want to encourage you to learn to participate and then accelerate your income by investing in real estate, the stock market, and businesses. Here are the primary streams of income from the Second X: rent from real estate; profits from a business; dividends from stocks; interest from bonds and CDs; and royalties from songs, books, etc. The idea is that we want to position ourselves to start participating in investing and moving forward and building our wealth.

STEP 6:
EMANCIPATE

Once the asterisks start rolling and the Second X starts forming, you will get to this awesome step: emancipate. This means that you get to the point of financial freedom where you can live off of your assets. This means you are free from First X income—your job—if you so desire.

Now that I'm emancipated, so to speak, I don't need to have to a job. However, I love teaching. I love going to different parts of the world to work and teach. But the difference is that I no longer need to do these things for the money. I'm free to do them whether or not they're profitable because I'm emancipated. I have reached the point where I have the freedom to live off of my assets.

STEP 7:
DONATE

The seventh step to financial freedom is: donate. The word donate means that you give and invest 100 percent of your excess money to kingdom purposes and social causes. After achieving the Second X, we need to work toward the Third X. This is where we will be able to give 100 percent of our excess income to others in our lives. This includes donations, but it can also include investments.

You can actually make an annual return on investing in social causes. It's called "social impact investing." In social impact investing, you simply reallocate some of your assets to invest in social causes. But you don't do it for the money; you do it because it offers aid and empowerment to the people you're helping. It will empower them instead of just enabling them. This is what I do through my nonprofit, Tricord Global.

Then He spoke a parable to them, saying: The ground of a certain rich man yielded plentifully. And he thought within himself, saying, "What shall I do, since I have no

room to store my crops?" So he said, "I will do this: I will pull down my barns and build greater, and there I will store all my crops and my goods. And I will say to my soul, 'Soul, you have many goods laid up for many years; take your ease; eat, drink, and be merry.'" But God said to him, "Fool! This night your soul will be required of you; then whose will those things be which you have provided?" Then Jesus said, "So is he who lays up treasure for himself, and is not rich toward God."

—Luke 12:26-21

The goal of the Third X is making sense of making money for making a difference. That's the vision statement for Wealthbuilders; it's the vision of this donate step. You position yourself financially, not just so you can build bigger barns, but so you can impact the kingdom!

SUMMARY

The first step is to escalate by increasing your ability to earn.

The second step is to eliminate consumer debt.

The third step is to accumulate. Now it's time to move forward. It's time to accumulate. This is the beginning of the Second X. At this step, we save for emergencies and start saving for a home.

The fourth step is to participate. Now that you've actively saved for a home, it's time to participate. Purchase your home, and open a Roth IRA.

The fifth step is to accelerate. There are three primary ways to accelerate: invest in real estate, invest in the stock market, and invest in your own business.

The sixth step is to emancipate. Once the asterisks start rolling and that Second X starts forming, then you get to this awesome step. This means that you get to the point of financial freedom where you can live off of your assets.

The seventh step is to donate. Donate means you give and invest 100 percent of your excess money to kingdom purposes and social causes.

PART TWO:
THE OTHER INGREDIENTS
AND MIXING THE BATTER

CHAPTER FIVE:

FOUR STEPS TO THE FIRST X

For most people in the U.S., there are really only two classifications of income according to the IRS, the Internal Revenue Service. (In other countries, it's typically known as the Revenue of Authority.) These two classifications are: earned income and passive income.

The tax authorities classify First X income, money you work for, as earned income. This is where, if you have a job and get paid, you are taxed according to earned income wages. Earned income wages come from you putting in time and value. A W-2 or a 1099 is issued for this type of earned income.

The second classification, Second X income, is passive income. The tax authorities classify passive income as income received from assets. For instance, these could be things like capital gains from a business, dividends from stocks, or rent from real estate property. If there's any positive cash flow from an asset, it is considered passive income not earned income.

Let's take a look at how this works when you own a business. The salary you get from the business is classified as earned income. But at the end of the year, you can take a capital distribution from that business, which counts as passive income. We'll cover passive income and the Second X in the next chapter, but for now, let's figure out how to master our earned income.

First X income is represented by the line of squares in the Triple X Factor, while the expenses are represented by the dots. The First

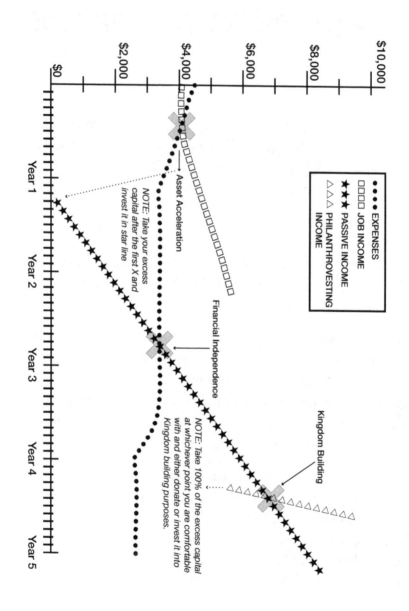

X is where those two intersect. Most people in the U.S. live right around the First X. In other words, they live off of their job.

So how exactly do we go about reaching the First X? How do we increase our First X Income and decrease our expenses? For most people, reaching the First X is going to be their starting goal in the Triple X Factor. Remember, the goal with building the First X is not to get a raise or find a better job—that's merely a step on the path of wealth building. The goal with building the First X is to reach a point of financial preparedness from which you can really start to build wealth. The point of reaching the First X is to put yourself in a position to truly build wealth, and remember, building wealth has little to do with your job. Now, let's take a closer look at the four steps to mastering the First X.

STEP 1: BECOME MORE VALUABLE

Jim Rohn said, "You are the average of the five people you spend the most time with." What he meant by this was that the more time you spend with people, the more you become like them. After time, you adopt their mannerisms, sayings, and ideas, until you become—in some sense—an average of these five people.

You can be pulled up or down by your associations. Now, this doesn't mean that you should go fire all your friends, but it may be time to branch out and make some new friends. For example, in America, there are some families in the sixth generation of welfare. They are living off of welfare because that is the only lifestyle they've ever known. Their environment is pulling them down instead of up.

Think about who you surround yourself with. Think about what those associations are doing to you. Do you influence each other for good? Do you better each other? Are you like iron sharpening iron?

As iron sharpens iron, so one person sharpens another.

Proverbs 27:17 (NIV)

Most people's wages fall within 20 percent of their friends' wages. So if you are looking to master your money, find some friends who have mastered theirs. Sometimes you need to be around people who can help pull you up. If you want to earn more or have a higher net worth, you should start befriending people who have already attained this. Then you will be in a position to learn from them, because true friends influence each other.

All of this boils down to the fact that in order to have an above-average income, you must become an above-average person. That's why it's important to invest in yourself more than you do in your job. As I stated earlier in this book, we get paid for our value not our time. Your company pays your salary because you hold a valuable position in the company, not because you show up from eight to five. Your time might be a part of that value, but it's not the whole part. Think about it: If you showed up from eight to five and did nothing, would you keep that job?

You really need to focus on increasing your value in order to increase your income. You become more valuable by investing in yourself. Learn to pour into yourself. Be, as Jesus said in Matthew 10:16, "Wise as serpents and innocent as doves." You will become more valuable when you learn to walk in the wisdom and the Word of God.

Three Actions for Investing in Yourself.

Learning. Try to read something positive and inspirational for 30 minutes every day. A good place to start is with the Bible. Through daily devotionals with God, you will be more valuable by becoming more of who God wants you to be. As the Holy Spirit speaks in your life and as you obey God, you will become more valuable to other people and to the kingdom of God.

You should also find a blogger whose vision you can really connect with or someone who knows a lot about something that you don't know a lot about. The Internet is full of free, great content from bloggers and businesses.

If you can, try to read two books a week. Now, most of us think, Goodnight, if I could read one book a month or even a year, I'd be doing well! I understand that people are busy and it might not be feasible to actually sit down and read a book, but could you listen to an audiobook, CD, mp3, iPhone app, or a podcast? Anything that will plant information in your heart and mind is going to educate you and help your development. The point is, if you do this, ten years from now you will have read either 1,000 books or listened to 1,000 programs. This will make a difference. And it will make you more valuable!

Listening. God uses the successful lives of other people to show us how to walk in excellence. When we see people who are successful, we can, by matching their beliefs and behavior, become successful ourselves.

Many people, however, have a difficult time learning from someone else. They think the other person must have an agenda, so they are unwilling to receive anything from them. In Hebrews 5:12, Paul scolded the Hebrew believers and said they needed someone to re-teach them the basics. He told them they were still in first grade because they were not willing to listen to anyone.

You can put yourself in a position to learn by finding someone you can trust. Listen to this person, even if his or her opinion runs counter to your own personal beliefs. If he or she is successful, and you are not, hindering beliefs are holding you back. A successful person's advice will help you grow and change, so follow it, even if it is uncomfortable and unfamiliar.

You may need help finding the right people, so ask God where to look. When Robert Schuller was getting ready to build the Crystal Cathedral, his construction estimate began at nine million dollars. (I believe the final cost of his project was considerably more than that.)

He went to one of his benefactors and asked him how to raise the money. The man replied, "How do you hunt a moose?"

Schuller said, "I don't know how to hunt a moose."

The man told him to go figure it out, and then he would have his solution. So when he got home, Schuller started thinking about it and said, "First of all, I must go where a moose lives. Second, I must learn the habits of a moose. Third, I'll have to learn what interests a moose. And fourth, I'd better be prepared when I hunt the moose." He then took those four guidelines and used them to raise millions of dollars for the Crystal Cathedral.

You need to ask yourself how to hunt a moose. If you are going to find someone who has been successful, go to where that person lives. The second thing you must do is learn the habits of that person. Third, decide what interests him or her. Fourth, be prepared when you go.

I once met for five uninterrupted hours with one of the greatest success authorities in the world. He came to speak at my church, and the next day, he spoke to twenty thousand people in a large arena. Other people asked me what I did to meet him. Well, I learned how to hunt a moose! I wrote him the kind of letter he would respond to, so not only did he come but he would not accept any money for speaking at my church.

When I met with him in private for five hours, I was prepared. I had a ten-page list of questions. I journaled all those answers, and today those answers are an invaluable resource to me. In some areas of my life, I learned more from him in five hours than I had learned in 20 years! Get around people who are doing something right. Learn what they are doing and why they are doing it, and you will be successful.

When my friend was battling cancer, we found a little book called *Healed of Cancer* by Dodie Osteen. Diagnosed with liver cancer, Dodie was told she had only three weeks to live. In her book, she gave us the recipe for getting healed. She showed us how to model her behavior and how to get what we needed from God. My friend did what she did, and he got the same results!

Some people have achieved a level of success, but do not even know what recipe they are using. They are like my wife's grandmother. My wife asked, "Grandma, how do you make those tea cakes?"

Grandma said, "I don't know."

Every Christmas we eat tea cakes, but Grandma does not know how she makes them. Finally, Grandma suggested, "Becky, why don't you come over and let me show you how to make those tea cakes?"

Becky went and watched. She asked, "Grandma, how much sugar do you put in?"

"I don't know, honey. I just reach in there with my hand and take this much out."

Becky watched as her Grandma took some sugar from the bowl. Then Becky put the sugar in a measuring cup to find the exact amount.

Grandma really did not know the recipe. She was almost 90 years old and had been making tea cakes for 80 years. Becky had to work to get the recipe!

Likewise, some people still don't know Dodie's recipe for her healing, even after reading her book. They still don't know what she actually did. They read that she meditated on the promises in the Bible, but she was not talking about meditating for ten minutes and then putting it down. She was talking about meditating in the Word all day long! When she talked about praying in the Spirit, she wasn't talking about only praying a few minutes, she was talking about praying all day!

You may say, "All day! But I have a family. I have to work. I have things to do." Dodie did not care what anyone else thought. She just locked herself in her bedroom and stayed there all day—praying and meditating. Few people know what that is like. They can't even imagine what it feels like.

If I had the opportunity to interview Dodie Osteen, I would ask questions to discover her recipe. I would ask, "What was your thinking process when the doctor said, 'You only have three weeks to live'? What pictures were you seeing in your mind at that moment? What pictures were you seeing in your mind after you went to the Bible? What were you feeling? What were you hearing? What new information was coming to you?"

Another thing I would ask Dodie Osteen is what beliefs she possessed at the time she heard her diagnosis. What did she believe about the process of meditating on and speaking the Word of God? I would ask, "When you were sitting in your bedroom on the fourth night after the doctor gave you three weeks to live, what were you believing about the process of faith?"

Most of us would be speaking affirmations of faith, but seeing pictures of ourselves dying. I would ask what pictures she was seeing. I would want to know what was in her mind. I once told a friend of mine, "I think the biggest thing she had that most people miss is that Dodie believed in the process of faith. Most people do not believe in the process, but she did. If you will operate in the process of faith, it will work every time—but you must find that process!

My son is a baseball pitcher at a NCAA Division One university. I told him, "When you get around guys who are successful and are making it to the pros, don't ask them how they throw a curve ball. Granted, that will help you, but there are other questions you can ask that will help you a lot more. Ask them what is going on in their mind when they are on the pitcher's mound. Ask them what they are feeling, thinking, and seeing. Get their recipes!"

Craig Maddox, one of the greatest professional baseball pitchers in all of history, has neither the physical stature nor the arm speed to be as successful as he is. He is successful because he knows how to *cut up* a batter, not because he knows the little tricks of the trade. He has success because he has a specific recipe when he gets on the mound.

If you want to be wealthy, take a rich person to dinner and ask him or her these questions. What do you believe about wealth? What kinds of things were you believing and thinking when you got started? What images were you seeing? What were you feeling?

Some of you want to see your teenager come back home; some want to see your marriage restored. But what images are you seeing? What are you picturing in your mind? What are you hearing and feeling? What are you believing?

I am giving you a strategy to discover the recipe. I know the Bible says that "faith comes by hearing, and hearing by the Word of God" (Romans 10: 17), but you need to know what people did with the Word of God to make it work for them.

Many people get depressed and ask, "Why is this happening to me?" Instead, they should be asking, "What can I do about it? What does God want me to do about it? What can God help me learn in the process of overcoming this? How can I beat this?"

The real question in the case of Dodie Osteen was not how long she could live, but how well she could act until her healing manifested itself. She set an amazing example for us as believers who desire change. And thanks to her, my friend had someone to imitate, and it's working for him too!

Find someone who will coach, teach, train, and mentor you, and then listen to them. I have always suggested that a poor person should take a rich person out to dinner, pay for a six-course meal, and just listen to them. But if you cannot afford a six-course meal, just ask them out for coffee. Let them talk while you just sit there and listen. The things you learn will be invaluable!

If you see a person you admire or whose life you envy, offer to take him out so you can hear about how he got to where he is. Come with a list of questions to get the most out of your time together. Ask what attributed to his success and how he got to where he is today. You can even ask if he would be willing to mentor you.

Looking. Success leaves clues. One of the greatest mistakes I made as a young man was assuming how and why people came into success, without ever really studying the successful people in my life. By looking and allowing God to teach us, we can learn to model people's examples. Paul said in 1 Corinthians 11:1, "Imitate me, just as I also imitate Christ." As we look and observe, we will start to see how people function and operate. Then we can imitate them.

One of the very first qualified mentors I had in real estate gave me a secret on how to find out if someone is going to be a good tenant. He told me that one of the best ways to qualify tenants is to see where they live (when possible) before they rent from you.

I asked, "How can I go see where they live?" He told me to take the lease to their house without telling them I was coming. Then when they let you inside, you get to see how they've kept their house. My mentor had owned rental property for 40 years, so he knew something about what he was doing. I just had to learn to humble myself and observe and imitate him.

You bring value to the marketplace, but there's always a way to increase that value. When building the First X, increasing your value is the first thing you should focus on.

STEP 2:
LEARN TO LIVE ON 80 PERCENT

The second step is to learn to live on 80 percent of your income, and honestly, I would challenge you to live on 70 percent of your income if you can. I realize that's not immediately possible for most people, but that's something to work toward.

So you may ask, "How does this work?" Well, the 80 percent goes to your expenses: debts, rent, food, fun, etc. Then you tithe 10 percent, put 5 percent with someone who can professionally invest the money and then personally invest the other 5 percent. (If you live on 70 percent, it looks like this: 10 percent to tithe, 10 percent to professional investor and 10 percent to personally invest.)

A mandatory withdrawal starts at the age of 70 for many Americans' 401k's and IRA's. And often, that mandatory withdrawal is taxed at the earned income tax rate. So what happens is that these people end up paying more in taxes when they retire than when they were actually working.

Instead of that, I recommend taking 5 percent and putting it into a Roth IRA or a mutual fund. But don't just professionally invest. Take 5 percent of your income in the beginning and learn how to invest it yourself. Do not only professionally invest it.

I started teaching my grandson how to personally invest when he was eight years old. I pulled him aside and said, "Brayden, listen, Poppa is going to teach you how to invest." So we went out on a Saturday morning and found a garage sale that had an old, broken-down, red wagon. It was rusted over and missing a wheel. We paid $2 for that broken wagon.

We took the wagon home, and I found some black and red paint in my garage. We bought a new wheel. I let Brayden do a lot of the sanding and some of the painting. When it looked like new again, we put a sign out in the driveway, and put the wagon up for sale. We sold it for $20. We had taken $2 and turned it into $20!

Of course, we had some costs with paint and a wheel, along with a lot of elbow grease. We put in a lot of sweat and equity, but Brayden walked away from that experience knowing how to invest.

This is a simple example of how you can personally invest. Find ways to bring in extra income by learning to personally invest in something. This could be a Mary Kay business or an eBay shop or flipping cars.

When you learn to live on 80 percent of your income, you are practicing mastering your money. It's going to be difficult to set aside those funds at first, especially when you're used to spending that money. It's actually going to require you to start mastering yourself in order to set aside these funds. But through this, you will learn self-control and discipline. And when you learn these things, you will be in a stronger position to start building wealth. You've just got to dig the trench!

I realize that for most people living on 80 percent of their income is nearly impossible immediately. But if you're serious about money mastery, you can grow to learn to live on even 70 percent—especially if you're taking value to the marketplace. And if your income is increasing, that 70 percent or 80 percent will increase as well.

STEP 3:
KNOW THE DIFFERENCE BETWEEN
ASSETS AND LIABILITIES

It's also important to learn to carefully manage that 80 percent of your income, and part of that is learning the difference between assets and liabilities. For example, when you buy a flat screen TV or a nice sports car, what happens to the value of that item when you take it out of the store? Its value depreciates immediately! It immediately becomes worth less than what you paid for it. These objectsare liabilities.

Here's what's amazing to me. People will walk into an electronics store and think nothing of putting $1,500 on credit to buy a flat screen TV. But when I challenge them to put $2,500 or $3,000 down to buy a $100,000 house, they say, "I'm not going to get in debt." Yet, they think nothing of buying a sports car on credit—even though the moment they drive it off the lot, its value depreciates. And the minute they walk out of the store, carrying that ginormous TV and put in the back of their pickup, its value depreciates as well.

I remember when I was younger and we didn't have flat screen TVs. We had these monster TVs. I mean, you had to have a crane to carry one. The first time I bought a TV for our family, I bought it on credit, and I remember I paid right around $450. So here I was, proudly trying to get this $450 gigantic boat anchor that we call a TV into the trunk of my car—all the while not realizing that its' value was depreciating with every passing second. It was a liability: an expense that does not pay you back.

Assets, however, are completely different. They are things like stocks, real estate, or businesses. Assets actually bring money to you. The idea is that as the assets bring you money, you can send that money out to your expenses and liabilities. There's nothing wrong with buying an engagement ring or a TV or a sports car. But what if you bought it with cash from assets instead of buying it on credit?

When you work on building the Second X, you reach a place of having income from assets. This is the cash you could be spending on liabilities. A liability is money that is paid to someone else; an asset is money that is paid to you.

You have to eat food to be able to exist and live, but food is a big expense. There are other needs like this in our lives that are big expenses. We need certain things. The issue, most of the time, is not that something costs too much. The issue is that you can't afford it.

Let's take an example based on a typical U.S. household and look at a simple asset statement. Say someone has cash savings of $7,500, a retirement account of $25,000, personal property (furniture, cars, etc.) of $50,000 and personal real estate of $200,000 (typically their home). They have no assets or real estate investments or insurance (annuity type assets) or equity in business or stocks and bonds. This would represent a typical family, with total assets of $282,500.

If we look at their liabilities, we see that they owe $20,000 on their personal property, which includes things like a $1,500 TV. They have personal real estate (mortgage on their house) of $150,000, credit card debt of $10,000, school loans (which are an epidemic in the U.S. right now) of $8,000 and miscellaneous debt of $3,000. So in total liabilities they have $191,000.

This very simple financial statement helps us find the net worth of a person. Take the total assets and subtract out the total liabilities. This gives you a person's net worth. In this illustration, their net worth is $91,500.

I didn't always made wise choices when it came to finances. But if you are investing in yourself, then the older you get, the wiser you get. When you do fail and you are learning, you start to call it noble failure instead of just failure, and you move forward.

In 2014, The New York Times said the typical American household had been getting poorer. The inflation of adjusted net worth for the typical household was $87,992 in 2003. Ten years later, it was only $56,335. That's a 36 percent decline!

This tells you two things: (1) Probably, the value of a lot of assets went down (like in the Great Recession) and (2) People had to spend some of their assets in order to make it through the recession. This caused their net worth to decrease.

We thank God for what we have and apply wisdom to what we do. I remember the first time I actually hit the substantial net worth of a million dollars. That does something to you! And it's all by the grace of God. If you partner with God, you can reach a powerful net worth too.

Playing the net worth game requires a lot of wisdom and blessing. You hear Wall Street use the term "arbitrage" a lot. In the biggest sense, arbitrage simply means that you figured out how to hedge your bets so that you're acquiring something that's worth more than you're paying for it.

For instance, if I look at a piece of real estate, and I know, either by an income approach or by a comparable sales approach, that the property is worth $100,000. But say I know, for other reasons, that I can buy it for $70,000, I just increased my asset line.

If I borrow $70,000, I will have a total investment of $70,000, but the home is still worth $100,000 by comparable sales. I just increased my asset line by another $100,000, but I increased my net worth by $30,000 (take the $70,000 off). It's a bit of a game, but it's pretty enjoyable to continue growing your net worth. It just has to be done properly.

So when it comes to understanding the difference between assets and liabilities in the Triple X Factor, it looks like this: The asset column is represented by the asterisks. Those asterisks represent the

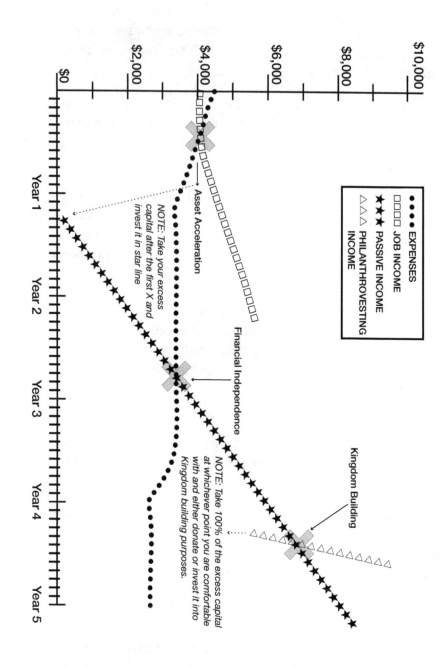

assets you hold as well as the income that comes from those assets. Liabilities are found in the asterisks.

The more you play the net worth game, the more your asterisks begins to escalate until they pass your dots. That's the point where you no longer have to work because you have reached financial independence.

STEP 4:
ELIMINATE DEBT

Consumer debt is one of the biggest plagues to us in western nations because of how easy it is to access. It has become a detriment to our nation.

I used to travel and speak with several personal finance teachers. These speakers would teach on debt elimination, which is a part of the First X, and I would teach on building the Second X and living out the Third X. That's how we shared the stage.

Many nights, we would stay up late, sharing our personal experiences and thoughts on wealth building, and honestly, a lot of the things I believe, I actually learned directly from these fellow speakers.

Let's look at a story of Person One and Person Two to illustrate our perspective on eliminating consumer debt. Person One earns $54,000 a year. He's lived in his home for five and a half years. He has paid off all of his debts, including his mortgage, his cars and credit cards in six years. (It is possible for most people to pay off all of their debt, including their home mortgage, in seven years by applying the principles listed below. Some can even do this in as little as five years, if their income line is high.)

After Person One is debt free, he invests the $2,500 a month he's been wasting on debt payments. He starts putting it into the asterisks, and twenty-four and a half years later, he owns his home, has no debt and has $3,200,000 in investments at a 10 percent average annual return. He's in a pretty good place!

Now, let's take Person Two, who also earns $54,000 a year. He's lived in his home five and a half years. He has continued to create and pay off debt. He makes his debt payments on time. He pays his mortgage out over decades, using standard payments. Person Two, twenty-four and a half years later, owns his home, but still has the same car debt, credit card debt and other debts. He has practically nothing to show in investments.

This story demonstrates how powerful getting out of debt can be. By simply reversing the direction of your money and investing it instead of spending it, you can end up in a really healthy place down the road. Yet, in America, we're taught how to be consumers. The word consume literally means "to destroy." So what are we destroying? Well, we are destroying our power to get wealth. Consuming keeps us from moving forward. How we spend money should truly reflect what matters to us.

In 1982, I read The Richest Man in Babylon, by George S. Clason. It's a powerful book that gives you a great basic understanding of finance. In this book, Clason says that you can spend 70 percent of what you make on anything you want as long as you properly manage the remaining 30 percent.

Now, it's okay to purchase things at or before the First X too. When living on the squares and the dots, it's still okay to purchase anything you want as long as you're doing it within the 80 percent or 70 percent. That 80 percent is meant to cover your liabilities.

Listening to Clason's advice, however, is even better. If you learn to live on the 80 percent and start building the asterisks, don't start buying real toys until you can pay for them from the asterisks. With a little patience, you'll be in a place of freedom when it comes to finances.

So how does consuming destroy our power to get wealth? For instance, if you purchase a $2,000 TV with a typical credit card, it will take 31 years and 2 months to pay off the balance by making the minimum payment. Read the fine print. You will end up paying a total of $10,202 for a $2,000 TV. That's $8,202 in interest alone at a 19.8 percent interest rate! So here's the question. What do you think that TV will look like 31 years later?

Now let's take a look at a conservative mortgage for a more aggressive illustration. Say there's a $275,000 property with a 30-year mortgage at 5 percent. If you run these numbers on an amortization schedule, you will find that you will end up paying $531,453 on a $275,000 mortgage. That's $256,453 in interest!

This illustration shows you the power of interest and how it can work against you.

> **Any enterprise is built by wise planning, becomes strong through common sense, and profits wonderfully by keeping abreast of the facts.**
>
> Proverbs 24:3-4 (TLB)

Debt elimination is important because most people in the U.S. are shackled to debt. Debt prevents us from building wealth. Too many people live their lives buried under consumer debt. We need to learn to break free and become the masters of our money!

According to Nerdwallet.com, as of 2014, American consumers are 11.62 trillion dollars in debt. Debt is oppressive and can snowball quickly. Today is the day to start tackling your personal debt. You can stop that snowball and roll it the other way by following a program I learned from those debt free elimination teachers who used to speak with me. It helps people get out of debt and into wealth in nine steps.

NINE STEPS TO GET OUT OF DEBT AND INTO WEALTH

Step 1: Cut up or freeze all but one credit card.

Break out the scissors and destroy those credit cards. Just keep one card! You need to keep that one card because you want to keep the credit lines open. Then, literally, get a metal coffee can, fill it with water, place that card into the can and stick it in your freezer! It has to be metal so you can't microwave it. By the time the water has melted, hopefully the desire to use the credit card for an impulsive purchase will have passed. You'll have time to think through the decision.

Do whatever it takes to make yourself stop using the cards as an excuse to bury yourself in debt. However, don't cancel your accounts because that will affect your credit score greatly. Instead, stop using the accounts and pay them off. This will improve your score.

Step 2: Pay off current charges every month or stop using the card altogether.

If you decide not to freeze that last card, you need to get serious. You can keep using it, but you need to make sure to pay off the current charges each month (and even better, switch to a debit card). The key here is to be religious. If you charge $200 on that card, then at the end of the month, you need to commit to pay that $200—not $10!

The following steps will be difficult if you don't learn to maintain this one. You really need to prevent further debt, while you move forward in eliminating debt.

Step 3: Make the minimum payment on all debts.

This is where the secret sauce starts. Don't be sporadic in your attack on debt. Start a rhythm. In a moment, I'll show you how to really accelerate this plan of attack. But for now, let's establish a base. Make the minimum payments regularly on all of your debt. It might take a little while to get into this rhythm, but it's your first real platform to reach in order to move forward in eliminating debt. Then you can start accelerating your debt eliminating process.

Step 4: List your current debts.

List your mortgage, car debt, credit card, school payment, etc. on a spreadsheet. List the debt, the balance, and your current monthly payment without the taxes and insurance. We just want to look at the hard number here. Next, divide the minimum monthly payment into the balance to find the number of months it would take to pay-off each debt.

Here's an example of what it might look like when you're done. This is a starting place for all of the following steps.

Step 5: Begin with debt paid off the most quickly using the minimum monthly payment.

The key here is how quickly the debt can be paid off, not how high the interest is. Most people start with the debt that has the highest interest, and because of that, they never seem to get ahead. So start with the debt that can be paid off in the shortest number of months. According to our sample debt list, that would be starting with Car 1. So we're going to tackle this debt with some oomph!

Back in our younger days before we knew anything about this debt plan, my wife sat down with a yellow legal pad and wrote out all of our expenses, including our debt. (By the way, my wife is the money manager in our relationship.) She then followed steps three

LIST YOUR CURRENT DEBTS

DEBT	BALANCE	PAYMENT	# OF MONTHS
Mortgage @ 6%	$139,000	$899.33	154
Car	$7,800	$522.65	14
Car 2	$21,500	$457.12	47
Credit Card 1	$2,250	$55.60	40
Credit Card 2	$1,850	$37.00	50
Home Equity	$18,700	$272.66	68

through five, just through intuition, and it was amazing what we were able to do through those steps! In nearly 11 months, she paid off everything we owed. She was able to accomplish this in a really short period of time because she used this principle.

You can do this too! Begin with the debt that can be paid off in the shortest number of months, not the one with the highest interest rate, and start knocking it off!

Step 6: Determine your winning percentage.

This is what will really help you kick your debt quickly. Your winning percentage is going to be the extra room in your budget. I talk a lot about living on 80 percent in light of eliminating consumer debt. Ideally, you'll be tithing 10 percent and investing 10 percent. But for people in heavy debt, it would be better to take the 10 percent that you would normally invest and use those funds as the winning percentage to get out of debt. In other words, you would tithe 10 percent and use 10 percent to get out of debt. And if you're living off of 70 percent, then keep investing 10 percent, but still make 10 percent your winning percentage. The point is to find a winning percentage that is not currently being used by your budget. So, what if you're living on 100 percent? Keep digging around in your budget until you find the ten percent or whatever your winning percentage may be.

Here are some questions to find your winning percentage (I'm sorry, but they're not the most fun): What can I sell? What expenses can I reduce or eliminate from my life? (Does the Latte Factor apply?) How can I earn extra money? Scrounge together a winning percentage. Getting out of debt is like digging trenches—it's hard work, but when it's done, the waters can flow.

Step 7: Apply your winning percentage to the debt that can be paid off the most quickly.

In this example, the debt that can be paid off the most quickly is Car 1, as it can be paid off (using the minimum monthly percentage) in 14 months. Now, we're going to take our winning percentage, 10 percent or $540, and add it to the minimum payment of $522. Now, you have an accelerated payment of over $1000 a month with an accelerated time frame of seven months. So instead of paying this particular debt off in 14 months, you can now pay it off in seven. That's half the amount of time!

Step 8: Once a debt is paid off, apply the total monthly payment to the next debt.

Now the snowball is really rolling. Now that the first debt is completely paid off, apply the total amount you were paying on the first debt to the next debt. Here's where we start cooking with grease. You've tackled your first, quickest debt, and now you're going to take the total monthly payment (winning percentage included) from that first debt and add it to the monthly minimum of the next debt that can be paid off the most quickly.

CAR 1

MONTHLY PAYMENT	$522.65
Winning percentage	$540.00
New Accelerated Payment	$1062.65
New # of Months	7
Old # of Months	14

Continuing with this example, you would take the accelerated payment from Car 1 and apply it to the next shortest debt: Credit Card 1. Credit Card 1's monthly minimum is $55.60, but we add the $1,062.65 from Car 1. This gives us a total accelerated payment of $1,118.25 per month. Now, we can pay Credit Card 1 off in less than two months. Instead of the snowball rolling you over, you're pushing it!

Basically, you are taking the money that you no longer have to pay towards your first debt and applying it to the next debt. And again, when that debt (Credit Card 1) is paid off, you take the total accelerated payment ($1,118.25) and apply it to the minimum monthly payment of the next shortest debt ($457.12 to get $1,575.37 per month), and then you repeat this pattern until you are debt free!

The numbers we're using here are real numbers. So this is doable! With this example, I got completely out of debt, including my home, in 84 months—seven years! You can do this, too!

Step 9: Apply your vastly increasing winning percentage to accumulating assets.

By this point, you will have a huge winning percentage. Take it and put it into accumulating assets. Now it's time to start moving toward the Second X. This part isn't often taught in debt-freedom programs, but the reality is debt freedom can't just be an end in itself. In addition to eliminating debt, you are working on bringing value to the marketplace and increasing your income. In seven years, you will become someone, but the question is: who?

You have to change your mindset concerning debt. Debt prevents you from being somebody; it prevents you from living with a purpose. When you get to the end of this program, take all that "free money" you've got lying around, since you're not paying off debts, and start putting it towards something. Start building your investment or passive income, what I call Second X income, by taking those funds and investing them in things like real estate, business, and stocks.

Start building wealth, and if you're like me, you want wealth because it gives you a platform to help change the world. Think about it: Why do you want to be debt-free? What is the main thing that keeps you in debt? What is your winning percentage? How will this freedom impact your dream?

A lot of people think that just because they're out of debt, they have nowhere else to go and nothing else to learn. They think that's the end, but the reality is, they are now simply in a position to start building wealth. Debt elimination is just the first step in the process

DEBT	BALANCE	ACCELERATED PAYMENT	# OF MONTHS
Car 1	$7,800	$1,062.65	7
Credit Card 1	$2,258	$1,118.25	2
Car 2	$21,500	$1,575.37	14
Credit Card 2	$1,850	$1,612.37	2
Home Equity	$18,700	$1,885.03	10
Mortgage	$139,000	$2,784.36	49
TOTAL			84

of building wealth.

We can't stop at eliminating debt. That's only the first of the three X's. We must continue to move ourselves into a position to acquire assets, build wealth, and play the net worth game. God brings us the treasures of darkness and the hidden riches of secret places. I want to challenge you to work hard on the First X, and from there, you can position yourself strongly to build the Second X.

SUMMARY

So how exactly do we go about reaching the First X? How do we increase our First X income and decrease our expenses? For most people, reaching the First X is going to be their starting goal in the Triple X Factor, and there are four steps to mastering it.

Step One to Building the First X: Become More Valuable. You can do this by 1) learning through reading and going through programs on a frequent basis, 2) listening by finding a mentor and friends from whom you can learn, and 3) looking by observing and questioning how people got to where they are. Success leaves clues.

Step Two to Building the First X: Learn to Live on 80 percent. That looks like 80 percent going to your expenses: debts, rent, food, fun, etc. Then you tithe 10 percent, put 5 percent with someone who can professionally invest the money, and then personally invest the other 5 percent.

Step Three to Building the First X: Know the Difference Between an Asset and a Liability. Liabilities, things like cars, jewelry, TV's, depreciate in value after you buy. They are worth less later. Assets, things like real estate, stocks and businesses, appreciate in value after you buy them. They are worth more later.

Step Four to Building the First X: Eliminate Debt. A friend of mine helped me develop our nine steps to getting out of debt. And the best part is that it ends with going beyond just eliminating debt and into building wealth!

CHAPTER SIX:

THE SECOND X, BUILDING WEALTH

With perseverance and patience, following those four steps will build the First X in your life. Your income line and your expense line will cross, and all of a sudden, you will have more income than expenses. This is where the wealth ball really starts rolling because you can take that excess income and begin aggressively investing it. This builds to the Second X—where you reach financial freedom.

Second X income, or asset income, comes from positive cash flow through marketable assets that increase in value over time. In other words, it's passive income. Building wealth, in this instance, looks like creating and gaining assets over a period of time. And if they are true assets, they should grow in value, thus increasing your Second X income.

An example of this would be someone getting a job right out of college. As they get older, their income will begin to increase because they have more knowledge and experience. They are getting paid for this because they are taking value to the marketplace. Properly managed assets do the same thing.

The asterisks represent Second X income. It increases for the same reason the line of squares increases: growth and increase in value. So how do we start the line?

After some time, dedication, and application of the four steps, you will create the First X. You will start to have a gap between

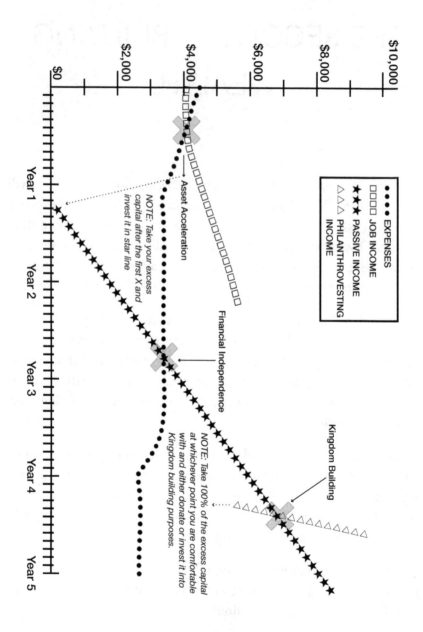

your expenses and income. Then you can take that excess capital and move it to start the asterisks. You can do this by investing the capital in that gap into assets. Then you will gain more assets, and your assets will increase in value. That's how wealth happens.

So what are examples of assets? True assets include: rent from real estate, profits from a business, capital distributions from a business, dividends from stocks, royalties from songs and books, interest from bonds, interest from CDs, etc. (When you buy Bonds and CDs, you have a certain interest rate that you get paid. This is called fixed income.) These are the primary areas of income-producing assets.

These assets are the place to start. I always personally recommend starting with rent from real estate, as it is typically the easiest to get into. Other places to start can be commissions from insurance, earnings from the Internet, and income from multi-level marketing. Sometimes, however, those three options will fall into earned income, instead of passive income.

Wealth building is fairly simple—it's just not easy. It takes a lot of energy and effort. It requires you positioning yourself properly. It begins with learning how to develop the First X and then moving on to build assets.

Mellody Hobson, as profiled in a 2008 issue of Money Magazine, summed this idea up well by saying: "When I was 22, a friend who is very successful explained to me that no one ever got rich through earned income. 'Look at all the great wealthy families,' he said. 'From Carnegie to Rockefeller, it was never how much they made at work that made them wealthy—it was their investments.' And that made me shift from thinking about a paycheck to thinking about building equity and long-term wealth. And it has helped me a lot. Instead of a raise, I ask for more stock."

THE RIGHT ATTITUDES

Building the Second X requires the right mindset or attitude. Having wrong attitudes can prevent you from making the changes you desire in your life. Wrong attitudes can hinder you financially. They can hinder your relationships. They can hinder your ability to make progress on your job. They can hinder every area of your life. Your attitudes can make or break you. They can propel you toward success or drag you to defeat.

What is an attitude? An attitude is what you really believe about something down deep inside. Your attitudes are determined by your belief system. What you believe about something in your life will determine how you feel about it. Attitudes determine how we approach everything in life.

For example, when my kids would come home from college, they would talk to me about problems they were having in their social lives or with their self-esteem. I would always tell them, "I see you need an attitude adjustment." Then I would talk to them about why they believe what they believe. I wanted to help them change how they were feeling about certain situations, and the only way I could do that was by helping them identify their wrong beliefs about those situations. As soon as they changed their beliefs, their attitudes would change as well.

If you focus on developing correct attitudes, you will have greater levels of success in developing the Second X. Now let's take a look at seven attitudes we should adopt in order to excel in wealth building.

ACCEPT PERSONAL RESPONSIBILITY

Have you ever caught your children doing something wrong? Kids have a tendency to shift the blame. If you catch them with their hand in the cookie jar, they will try to blame someone else. They might even blame you for making such good cookies!

Many adults, unfortunately, also suffer from this blame-shifting syndrome. Many people lose interest in transformation when they find out they are personally responsible for making it happen. This is especially evident with married couples who are experiencing a lot of conflict in their marriage. Each spouse wants the other to change, yet neither one realizes that in order to see the changes that they desire in their mate, they must change first. When I give this advice to married couples, the typical response is, "Why do I always have to be the one to change?" My answer is always that change is your responsibility.

For example, putting gas into a car will not make it start if it has no spark plugs. You can blame the gas station for selling bad gasoline or the car manufacturer for producing an inferior product, but the reality is that you need to take responsibility and have the spark plugs installed. People try to blame everyone and everything for their problems, but the truth is that in order for your circumstances to change, you must change!

An old African-American hymn says it best, "It's not my brother or my sister, but it's me, 0 Lord, standing in the need of prayer." Accepting personal responsibility is the highest form of human maturity. You are where you are due to the choices you have made. There are exceptions to that, of course, because you cannot control everything that happens to you. You can, however, always control your response. For instance, you cannot control the fact that a tornado tore down your house, but you can control how you react to the situation.

In Mark 9, the Bible tells the story of a father with a sick child. The father asked Jesus if there was anything He could do. Jesus answered him, "If you can believe, all things are possible to him who believes (9:23)." Another version of his answer might be, "What do you mean if I can do anything? All things are possible to you when you believe."

Jesus put the responsibility for the son's getting wellness right back on the man. That may seem unfair, but it effectively illustrates the vital part you play in changing the condition of your own life. You cannot remove yourself from the change process. You are responsible for doing what you can in order to change your circumstances.

If you are having problems with your teenager, you are responsible for doing what you can to bring about change. You can say, "I don't have any influence. I can't control what my teenagers do when they're not in my presence." Maybe not but you can make creative decisions about how you are going to deal with their actions. You can make creative decisions about providing appropriate consequences. You can make creative decisions about gaining new knowledge and getting outside help if necessary.

Then as you choose these appropriate responses, your teen's behavior will begin to turn slowly, like a large ship, in the direction you desire it to go. You may not be able to change the destination at the moment, but you certainly can change the direction. If you cannot change things inside the boat, at least you can influence the direction the boat is heading!

For example, a minister discovered that his teenager was experimenting with drugs. He attempted to talk with his son but could not get through to him. The minister was at the end of his rope. He spent some time alone, praying and asking God what to do. A drastic answer came to his mind: He should take a leave of absence from his church and do whatever was necessary to reach his boy.

The minister decided to change their environment. He had been totally caught up in the environment of his church, and his son had been totally caught up in the environment of his drug-using friends. He made a dramatic decision to take his son on a shrimp boat that remained at sea for three months. This way, neither he nor his son could leave the company of one another.

The results were staggering! By choosing to change their environment, the minister and his son were able to reconnect without any outside interference. The son later said that when his father took a leave of absence, he knew that his father loved him unconditionally.

I spoke with this minister before and after the trip, and it was apparent to me that he took complete responsibility for his son's problem. Yes, the son had to choose to change, but it was the father's actions and attitude of personal responsibility that encouraged the son's positive choice.

You cannot always control your problems, but you can always control how your problems affect you. You select the direction you desire to go. When a person determines not to be swept along on the currents of life but chooses to swim upstream instead, he is assuming responsibility for reaching a chosen destination. You are responsible for your direction and destination in life, regardless of the opposition.

Remember that if things are going to change, you must change. You have to be willing to give up all your excuses. Some people go through their entire lives blaming others. They say, "I drink because my dad treated me badly when I was a kid." That may be true, and he may have had a very negative influence on you, but now you are a grown person with the power to choose. You must accept responsibility and quit allowing yourself to play the victim. Personal responsibility is the key for any major change to take place in your life.

You may not be able to change the destination of your money at this very moment, but you certainly can change the direction. You have the power to select the direction you desire to go. No excuses. Don't blame someone else for your financial situation. Don't say, "I'm poor because my parents didn't teach me to manage money." Whether or not that's true, you now have the power to choose what happens next. By accepting personal responsibility, you take hold of the steering wheel to wealth building.

TAKE PERSONAL CONTROL

Once you've accepted responsibility, it's time to take control. Making a personal choice about what you are going to do with your life is the single most independent thing you can do. God gave you the power of choice so you could take personal control.

We all have seen teenagers try to model themselves after someone else. Most teenagers want to do their own thing, yet they end up doing the same thing as the rest of their peers. They are influenced by someone else's perception of cool. For instance, one time I encountered a teen once who was wearing what appeared to be a logging chain. The links were three inches in diameter, and he had to lean backwards to keep from falling over!

The truth is, we never stop being influenced by someone else's standards. As adults, we are still constantly bombarded with messages to be, think, or look a certain way. No one lives in a vacuum. Outside influences are perpetually trying to mold us. For instance, our society tries to convince us that credit card debt is normal. And hey, you get 3 percent back!

You must take personal control of your life and refuse to be ruled by somebody else's opinion. Miracles can happen when a person makes the decision to stand up and say, "No, I'm not going along with the crowd. I'm going to do things differently." Against all odds, that person will succeed!

Your experiences in life are determined by your choices. If you fall into bankruptcy, you can choose whether or not to accept it. It may not be easy; it may not be automatic. And it will definitely not be without a fight! But you can choose. You have a right to make these choices—and you have more control than you think!

EXPECT THE BEST

The next attitude necessary for personal change is expectancy of the best. What are your expectations concerning wealth? Are they negative or positive? You can't have the attitude of expecting the best and walk around depressed. It's impossible!

Expecting the best is as simple as making a decision to see your future in a positive light. When you are looking forward to something, you have hope. Paul said he was "looking for the blessed hope and glorious appearing of our great God and Savior Jesus Christ" (Titus 2:13). In other words, he was expecting the best for his future.

When you are looking forward to something, you have hope. Some people are constantly looking for every negative, disabling event that can possibly happen, and they find them! But, Paul said that he was looking for the best. Like Paul, we should be looking forward to spending eternity with God, but we should also be looking forward to fulfilling the dreams we have in this life. Stress comes into your life when you do not have anything to look forward to. Even if it's something as simple as going to Starbucks to get a cup of coffee, it has to be something you look forward to. Find something you want to experience, and do it! Always give yourself something to anticipate.

I once told a board member of a certain church, "The best investment you can make is to give your pastor something to start looking forward to."

He asked, "What do you mean?"

I then proceeded to share with him how my church had sent me to Hawaii several years before and how that Hawaiian vacation had broken a depressed pattern I had been experiencing for months. First, it gave me something to look forward to, and second, the change in my environment proved beneficial for me personally, as well as for my congregation.

In the Nazi concentration camps of World War II, when the Germans were killing Jews by the millions, a professor by the name of Victor Frankel witnessed the atrocities first hand. He wrote about his experiences in those concentration camps. One of the things he said had enabled him to deal with such horror was the fact that he could imagine himself teaching again. In his mind, he could see himself standing at the podium lecturing. He could also see his students.

He knew escape was not probable, yet the pictures in his imagination gave him something to look forward to. He began to expect the best for his life, and it galvanized his determination to live.

He survived the concentration camps and eventually made it back into the classroom. Later, he wrote the classic book Man's Search for Meaning. In this book, he shared things he learned from that terrible situation. He creatively expected the best. Therefore, he was able to prevail.

We must have an attitude of expecting the best. Most people don't expect the best because they have been disappointed once too often. Disappointing things happen to us all, but we cannot allow those things to cause us to bury our heads in the sand. We must be willing to keep expecting.

I like to have three or four things that I am expecting the best about at any given time. I expect the best with my family.. I expect the best with my businesses. And I expect the best with my finances. I always write down my expectations so that I will have something to be excited about at all times.

When my friend was diagnosed with cancer, I encouraged him to start expecting the best by visualizing himself doing something he really loved. For him, that was bicycle touring. He enjoyed high-tech bikes that were sleek and expensive. He and his doctor hit it off talking about the sport. As they began to discuss specific types of bicycles and upcoming tours, the focus was no longer on his illness but on something that excited him. He began to look forward to the day when he would again be able to participate in certain tours.

When a doctor says, "You have cancer, and now I'm going to give you every gory detail," your focus must be on something positive. Doctors do that because they do not want you to live in denial, but expecting the best is very different from living in denial.

My friend did not deny that he had cancer; he just chose not to focus on it. Instead, he began to build an image inside himself of what it would feel like to tour again. He built an image of life and hope for his future. It changed his focus, and during the writing of this book, he has participated in several bike tours.

To help develop an attitude of expecting the best, ponder these questions: What images am I presently concentrating on in my mind? What images can I focus on that will motivate me to expect the best? What choices am I intentionally making that ensure my present attitude stays empowering rather than defeating?

Do whatever you need to do to change your present attitude. When you see positive results, you will be glad you did!

BE WILLING TO BE CREATIVE

The next step is a willingness to be creative. Maybe you feel stuck or trapped in your current financial situation. Maybe you have some bad habits that you have never been able to break. Or perhaps, you think, I'm never going to change.

You need to be creative. No matter where you are right now, there is a strategy that will enable you to move forward. Being creative is the most God-like thing you can do. God is the ultimate creator. He sat on the edge of nothingness and told the light, planets, sun, and moon to exist. He had a blueprint inside Himself of what He wanted this universe to look like, and He spoke out what He saw. God has given you an imagination like His so that you can speak out the things you imagine for your own life.

History is filled with people who dared to imagine physical things that had never before existed. These dreamers and inventors were laughed at by those who declared their ideas impossible. Yet, many of those ideas have become the inventions that we enjoy today, such as the light bulb and telephone. They only became realities because these dreamers were willing to exercise their imaginations.

People have strong tendencies to doubt their own creativity, especially when they are trying to imagine a way out of their current situation. But there is always a way for you to get where you need to go. When you really believe there is a way for you to lay hold of the changes you desire, you will become willing to be creative.

For instance, my mother was a stubborn woman. All her life, she resisted being pressed into someone else's mold. She faced many challenges in her health, and many times she refused to respond in the manner the doctors thought she should. She was willing to be creative. If the doctors told her she could not walk, she walked. If they told her she could not get out of bed, she got out of bed. I'm not telling you to be irresponsible; I'm merely pointing out that nothing can confine you to your present circumstances if you are willing to be creative and partner with God.

HAVE CONFIDENCE TO DESIGN YOUR FUTURE

To design your own future, you have to identify your own priorities and values. You have to determine the things that are meaningful to you. You need to be willing to call the shots in your life. You have to be willing to pick up the pen and compose an ending to your own story.

Have you ever asked yourself, "What is important to me?" Too many of us are living our lives for someone else, for another human being. In order to design your own future, you must not be limited by what other people think. If you are trying to build wealth for someone else, the change probably will not last. You have to choose your own changes for your own reasons.

You also need to identify your purpose. One time, I was teaching at a seminar when the CFO of a company asked me how he could find his purpose in life. I told him that his purpose would be revealed when he identified what he desired in life and gave specific direction to those desires. Your purpose is your identified values expressed through your written goals.

When some people try to define their purpose, they do not consider their core values. They usually only think of two groups of surface desires. The first group they consider is that which will take them out of their immediate problems, and the second group of desires is primarily money-related. Even though these desires are significant, people never go beyond these desires and reach to their core values.

You have to discover your core values before you can identify your true desires. You have to discover your ultimate goal in building wealth before you can truly build wealth. To help determine what is most significant to you, ask yourself these questions: What would I do with my life if money were not an issue? What do I want my tombstone to say about me? What am I doing with my life that will live on after I die?

Your purpose becomes the strongest incentive in making the necessary changes in your life. Your purpose is like your physical appetite, except it functions on a spiritual level. Your appetite moves you effortlessly toward food, just as your purpose moves you toward the changes you need to make in order to fulfill your potential. When you meet resistance, your purpose will push you forward.

Next, in order to have confidence in designing your future, you must ask for the things you desire. This may sound simplistic, but many dreams have gone unfulfilled because someone failed to ask. The Bible tells us that if we ask, we will receive (Matthew 7:8). That is a powerful formula. Yet many people go through life without asking.

One of the best ways to ask is to write out everything you want as precisely as you can. Goals are like targets; precision tells you where to shoot. Most people, however, take the shotgun approach when it comes to getting what they want out of life. They just randomly shoot and hope they hit something.

As a youngster, I discovered that it was easy to shoot a shotgun and miss! One time, when I went dove hunting with a couple of friends, I shot two boxes of shells before I ever hit a bird. Doves fly fast, and your aim has to be precise in order to hit one. The same thing is true of your goals; you have to define them precisely if you want to hit your target.

Not only must you ask but you must be convinced that you can obtain your desires.

Whatever things you ask when you pray, believe you
receive them, and you will have them.

Mark 11:24

In other words, you must believe that you are in possession of
your goals before you ever obtain them. How do you do that? The
answer is to use your sixth sense of faith. For instance, have you ever
been desperately thirsty and gulped down a bottle of ice-cold min-
eral water? If so, you have some idea of how faith works. The sensations you experienced when you drank that water were incredible.
The refreshment you felt was unbelievable. Your sense of touch and
taste became incredibly alive.

Faith works the same way, except it operates in the spiritual
dimension. Faith causes you to experience the sensations of having
obtained your desires before you reach them. The sensations of faith
are so real that you feel like you are already in possession of your
goals before you actually reach them. As a matter of fact, when you
do reach them, it is no big deal because you have already been experiencing what it is like to have them! You can apply this principle of
faith to any desired change.

When you experience the sensations of change before you actually possess that change, you believe your personal transformation is
possible regardless of the obstacles you face.

LEARN TO TAKE ACTION

Another attitude necessary for personal change is learning to
take action. Just beginning to take action is 50 percent of accomplishing the action. Many people see what they need to accomplish,

think about where they need to go, dream about the possibilities, but never take any action.

For as the body without the spirit is dead, so faith without works is dead also.

James 2:26

Change only occurs when you begin to take action toward your desired goal. The actions you take must be harmonious with the outcome you desire. If you say you want to lose weight but keep visiting Dairy Queen, your actions are not in harmony with the outcome you desire. As a matter of fact, they are taking you in a direction contrary to where you want to go! You must bring your behavior in line with your desired change. If you can do this, you will be successful in any change you undertake.

Your actions must also be unwavering in nature. Harmonious actions amplify each other, enabling you to become even stronger in the direction you desire. Physical exercise is a good example of a harmonious action, because the more you develop your muscles through constant use, the easier it becomes to do certain exercises.

You are imprinting the desired change into your mind and body by repeating the desired behavior over and over.

For example, have you ever driven to work and then forgotten how you got there? If so, it's because the path to your workplace is so entrenched in your mind that you arrive there with very little conscious thought. Many areas of our lives are the same way. We often find ourselves performing self-defeating behaviors as though we are on auto-pilot. The good news, however, is that you can imprint self-enhancing behaviors on your mind in the same way. The more often you repeat a certain behavior—doing it over and over again—the more ingrained it will become. Then, over a period of time, the positive behavior will be executed almost unconsciously.

ADAPT TO SUCCEED

The last attitude you need to develop is adapting to succeed. There are two ideas you need to grasp in order to understand this concept. First, if you do not enjoy the results you are getting in life, change what you are doing. In order for things to change, you must change. Someone once defined insanity as doing the same thing, over and over again, while expecting different results!

If you bounce a ball the same way every time, it will respond accordingly. If you bounce it harder or softer, you will get different results. Likewise, in order for you to adapt, you need to watch the outcomes you are getting from the actions you are taking. Then you must be willing to change your actions if you are not obtaining your desired results.

Second, you must be flexible in changing times. Some people do not change with the times and get left behind. This happened to the railroad companies in the earlier part of the twentieth century. They believed that they were in the train business instead of the transportation business. Due to this faulty belief, they failed to make the necessary changes that would have allowed them to keep up with the changing times. Personally, I am fascinated with trains, but if I have to travel from Denver to New York, I take a jet!

Things have changed a lot in the last two decades. The introduction of the Internet and e-commerce is drastically changing how we live, shop, work and play. Companies and individuals that do not adapt to the times get left behind.

One of the purposes of this book is to help you develop the attitudes you need to adapt to the rapidly changing times in which we live. You can either stay stuck or you can grow. If you do not move forward, you can count on the fact that soon you will drift backward. If you concentrate on building the seven positive attitudes we have examined in this chapter, you will be ready to face any changes that come your way. You will be ready to face the process of building wealth.

HOVERING OVER THE FACE OF THE WATERS

Most people in America are taught how to earn money, save money, and get out of debt. But debt elimination is not the highest point of freedom, and until you are taught how to make money, you won't reach true financial freedom. You need to ask yourself the following questions: Where do I go after I am free from debt? And how do I get there? How do I start building the Second X?

You need to have the right attitude in order to change your mindset concerning wealth building. One of the things that thrills me about being able to provide micro-finance loans in developing countries with Tricord Global is that most people there don't have any means to earn money. There are so few opportunities for people in these poor nations to get jobs. They can only make money. In other words, they have to start at the Second X.

I'm connected to an American MBA program in Africa. After people graduate from that MBA program, they still cannot get a job in Africa because there aren't enough jobs for everyone. It's hard for us to understand that in the U.S. because we are a prosperous nation with lots of employment opportunities. Yet having lots of employment opportunities in America also lends itself to its own set of problems. People tend to keep themselves in a box since they can earn money. In other words, they don't think about making money.

For example, if I gave most people in the U.S. $1, would they be able to turn it into $2 dollars? For most people, the answer is no because they do not know how to build wealth. That's the reason we have such a challenge teaching the Second X in the U.S.

I believe in working. I work even though I don't need to. I do it because God's called me to do so. It's not that work isn't good; work is very good. But we need to learn how to make money and live off of our money in order to build wealth.

In the beginning God created the heavens and the earth. The earth was without form, and void; and darkness was on the face of the deep. And the Spirit of God was hovering over the face of the waters.

Genesis 1:1-2

This process of "hovering" is how God releases the creative process in you. It starts with God leading and guiding you. In this passage, we see that the Holy Spirit was brooding, or hovering, over the face of the waters. Out of that hovering, God said, "Let there be light." And out of that brooding, God began to create the heavens and earth.

How does this apply to you? Well, you have to take the time to learn and to think about what God wants you to do next. You have to spend some time brooding and hovering before you make a move.

Fifty percent in accomplishing anything is taking the first step. Some people say that's too simple, but if I get my feet in the water, I find that the water often begins to part. That's when God shows up and begins to guide you. You will begin to move forward in this creative process with Him. But first you've got to take that step of faith.

You also need to take an inventory of yourself. Take a look at your core competencies, your personality, your motivation, your tolerance for risk, your ability to deal with difficult people, etc. Use tools like Myers Briggs and Strengthsfinder to help you in this process.

Whatever personality test or personal inventory guide you choose to use, make sure that what you're reading and discovering hits your core. It's important for you to understand yourself. Don't allow your limitations to keep you from going where God wants you to go.

You can have an impact and partnership with God in the creative process to tikkun olam. You can help God take the mundane and elevate it to the holy. If there are limitations, always remember that with God all things are possible (Matthew 19:26). He is not limited by your limitations. If you believe that, you will be able to move to the place that God has for you.

Remember, you take value to the marketplace. So when you're building the Second X, it's very important that you continue to invest in yourself. Building the First X can be done in a series of steps, but building the Second and Third X is not quite as straight of a shot. Instead, there are many different routes and tools to building wealth at this level. While you may not be able to see exactly what the path looks like, you can learn the laws that will keep you on the right path. Just as you trust God to lead you when you can't see the way forward, you can trust the laws to lead you when you can't see the path ahead.

I can't tell you exactly how God is going to build wealth in your life. It may be through real estate like it was for me. Or it may be through stocks and bonds or business. Only you and the Lord can answer that question. Remember that God allows you time to hover before you jump into a new venture. He gives you time to plan, think, and get information before you start taking those steps. As you begin the process of gaining assets using the Four Laws of Wealth, take time to brood and pray over your motives and your plans.

SUMMARY

With perseverance and patience, your income line and your expense line will cross, and all of a sudden, you will have more income than expenses. This is where the wealth ball really starts rolling. Then you can take that excess income and begin aggressively investing it. This builds to the Second X—where you reach financial freedom.

Examples of Assets: True assets include things like rent from real estate, profits from a business, capital distributions from a business, dividends from stock, royalties from songs and books, interest from bonds, interest from CDs, etc.

Building the Second X requires the right mindset. Having the wrong attitude can hinder you financially because your attitude can make or break you.

Wealth-building attitudes include: accepting personal responsibility, taking personal control, expecting the best, being willing to be creative, having confidence to design your future, learning to take action and adapting to succeed.

Most people in America are taught how to earn money, save money, and get out of debt. But debt elimination is not the highest point of freedom, and until we are taught how to make money, we won't reach true financial freedom.

You have to take the time to learn and to think about what God wants you to do next. You have to spend some time brooding and hovering, before you make a move. Fifty percent of accomplishing anything is taking the first step.

You take value to the marketplace. When you're building the Second X, it's very important that you continue to invest in yourself.

CHAPTER SEVEN:

GOD'S LAWS OF WEALTH

Once you have put yourself in a position to start building wealth, there are four laws you can follow to get you all the way there. These laws of wealth pertain to the Second and Third X's. Throughout my life, as I've journeyed to build wealth, I have learned that the key is partnering with and obeying God. And it is only through working with Him that I've been able to identify these laws.

At this point of the Triple X Factor, you are still at the First X. You are still increasing your income and eliminating consumer debt, but you're starting to build assets. And when the income from those assets exceeds the amount of money that your expenses are costing you, you have reached the point of financial independence. These laws give you the framework for how to get to that point.

> Then you say in your heart; 'My power and the might of my hand have gained me this wealth.' And you shall remember the Lord your God for it is He who gives you the power to get wealth, that He may establish His covenant which he swore to your Fathers, as it is this day.
>
> Deuteronomy 8:17-18

We need to remember that it is the Lord who gives us the power to get wealth. He does this so that He may establish His covenant through us by using these laws of wealth. So what kind of laws does

God use when it pertains to wealth? How does God go about giving us the power to get wealth? Well, keep reading!

I call these four laws God's laws, because they specifically have to do with partnering with God. When we partner with God in these laws, He gives us the power to get wealth.

THE LAW OF CHANGE

'No one puts a piece from a new garment on an old one; otherwise the new makes a tear, and also the piece that was taken out of the new does not match the old. And no one puts new wine into old wineskins; or else the new wine will burst the wineskins and be spilled, and the wineskins will be ruined. But new wine must be put into new wineskins, and both are preserved. And no one, having drunk old wine, immediately desires new; for he says, 'The old is better.'

Luke 5:36-39

When there is new wine, we must offer God a new wineskin. This new wineskin we offer God is a renewed mind. It means that we must have a spirit ready to change.

As people begin to make progress in mastering money, they get into an area that is uncomfortable and unfamiliar. They start feeling a little funny on the inside and say, "Hmm…this doesn't feel right." It's like putting a shirt on that doesn't quite fit yet because it just needs to be stretched out a bit. But I've seen people make the mistake of thinking this discomfort is a sign. They think that the Holy Spirit is telling them to stop, and this misinterpretation of the Holy

Spirit's guidance prevents many people from moving forward and growing into what God has for them.

In 1978, I heard a story that really impacted my life. It's was about two men, Duane and Gary. Gary was watching Duane fish on a pier in California and began to notice something curious. Whenever Duane caught a big fish, he would throw it back into the ocean, but whenever he caught a smaller fish, he would put it into his fish bucket to take home.

Gary watched Duane for a while, but finally his curiosity got the best of him. He walked up to Duane and said, "Say sir, I've been watching you fish for a while, and it seems to me you're doing something a bit strange. Every time you catch a big fish, you throw it back, and every time you catch a small fish, you keep it. I'm just curious. Why you do that?"

Duane said, "Oh, that's easy. I've only got a 10-inch skillet at home!"

Sometimes we can't take the new wine—or the bigger fish—because we only have a 10-inch skillet. When we face challenges that we need to overcome in order to move forward, it's time for us to follow the law of change. We must be willing to leave behind what is familiar and comfortable.

In John 5, we read the story of the man at the pool of Bethesda. Jesus came to the man and asked him an incredibly important question. The man had been suffering for 38 years, which is an incredibly long time. So, Jesus asked him, "Do you want to be made well?"

This seems like a strange question to ask. But sometimes we get so familiar with our limitations, and so comfortable with our 10-inch skillet, that when somebody comes along and wants to help us get a new wineskin or a 16-inch skillet, we freeze. We feel uncomfortable.

If you are willing and obedient, you shall eat the good of the land.

Isaiah 1:19

Evidently, there were some people who weren't willing, and because of that, they didn't get to experience the blessing God had for them. That's the challenge we have in our lives, especially when we're at the First X. We have to be willing to grow and change.

Remember, every change begins with an ending. In order for you to change, something has to end in your life. For something to change, you must be issued a death certificate and a birth certificate at the same time. The death certificate is the passing of the old, and the birth certificate is the beginning of the new.

Most assuredly, I say to you, unless a grain of wheat falls into the ground and dies, it remains alone; but if it dies, it produces much grain.

John 12:24

I had a favorite food I used to eat all the time when I lived in Houston, Texas. Houston had a lot of rice farms so rice was a plentiful commodity. When I was a kid, my mother would fix white rice and cream gravy. Nowadays, we try to eat brown rice and get some fiber, but back then, we weren't concerned about health. That's why my favorite dish became white rice with cream gravy. Not brown gravy—cream gravy. Let me explain cream gravy to you.

The number one ingredient in a good cream gravy is grease, pure animal fat. Not vegetable oil, not olive oil, and certainly not extra virgin olive oil. I'm talking hardcore animal fat!

Now, this is a South Texas kind of meal. You melt the grease in a pan and add some flour. Then you pour some whole milk in and cook it until suddenly you have this absolutely outstanding (I'm telling you, put some salt and pepper on it, and it's perfect!) cream gravy.

I would put that cream gravy on top of some white rice, and then, just to make it heavenly, I would douse it all in Heinz ketchup. Yes, you read that right. I hate to admit it, but I could eat a bunch of the stuff. It was amazing!

When I began to get an understanding of the law of change, however, I actually had a funeral for rice and gravy. I took my minister's portable communion set and headed into the kitchen. True story. I stood in my kitchen and said, "In Jesus' name, I say rice and gravy is dead to me. I bury you in my life, in Jesus' name." Then I took communion.

But just a couple of weeks later when I came home after a hard day and walked in the back door, I heard rice and gravy call out to me from the grave, "Come and partake. Come and partake." I didn't, but that's the challenge we have when it comes to discarding an old wineskin and embracing a new one. Change isn't easy, and money mastery is one of the greatest challenges we face. By far, the vast majority of people are living just before the First X. They don't just start there, that's where they live and stay.

In order to move from the First X to the Second X, there must be the ability to move forward and change. We can change with God's help and power and embrace the things He has for us.

In the beginning of Deuteronomy, the nation of Israel was in the wilderness.

The Lord our God spoke to us in Horeb, saying: "You have dwelt long enough at this mountain. Turn and take your journey, and go to the mountains of the Amorites... See,

I have set the land before you; go in and possess the land which the Lord swore to your fathers..."

Deuteronomy 1:6-8

If you have been dwelling at that First X mountain, unable to move forward, it's time to change. If you just get to the First X, that's a good thing. That means you've increased your income, and you've either gotten completely out of debt or have greatly reduced your debt.

If you really want to get to that level—where God really empowers you to get wealth so that you can have an impact in the earth—then you've got to be willing to move on from the mountain you're at. And that's a big challenge!

It's going to take a true decision to change. Let's break that word down: "de" means "from," and "cision" means to "cut." So when I make a decision to change, it means I am cutting from where I am. In other words, I am cutting off the old. It's saying, "I've been at this mountain long enough, thank you. I'm going to go get a new skillet." When I make a decision, I cut from the old and embrace the new.

THE LAW OF WISDOM

The law of wisdom is one of my favorite laws to talk about because it's one of the most misunderstood.

Through skillful and godly Wisdom is a house (a life, a home, a family) built and by understanding it is established [on a sound and good foundation] and by knowledge shall its chambers [of every area] be filled with all precious and pleasant riches.

Proverbs 24:3-4, AMP

The Living Bible says it this way:

Any enterprise is built by wise planning, becomes strong through common sense, and profits wonderfully by keeping abreast of the facts.

This verse lists three primary qualities for profitable enterprise: knowledge, understanding, and wisdom.

The fear of the Lord is the beginning of knowledge.

Proverbs 1:7

Too often we disassociate the idea of having wisdom from the idea of obtaining knowledge. We think wisdom just happens, but we need a foundation of knowledge for wisdom to grow upon.

My people are destroyed for lack of knowledge.

Hosea 4:6

Unfortunately, I see people destroyed by a lack of knowledge all the time. They make the mistake of moving before understanding. In fact, I've made this mistake many times! But when it comes to obtaining knowledge, don't just ask what the cost is, ask about the worth.

I recently bought a $1,997 program to teach me about a specific area of business that I wanted to grow in—Internet marketing.

When I paid for that product, I felt good about the price because I knew I was going to get a lot out of it. I listened and learned. And then without any embellishment, made ten times what I paid for the program within two weeks' of applying the principles it!

I could have said, "Well, look how much that costs." Yes, $1,997 is a pricey fee. But the program was worth was a completely different number. It became worth a lot!

I'm not suggesting that you go out and flippantly throw money on a wall to see if it sticks, but I am suggesting that you need to understand how you're going to acquire knowledge and understanding.

Take this example for instance. Say I have a friend named Dave, and I tell him, "Dave, I found a gold mine, and you can dig up all the gold you want. Just go get a shovel!"

Dave replies, "Do you know how much they want for shovels? It's way too much!" Dave is allowing himself to be defeated by the cost of the shovel before processing through what the worth of that shovel would be. But in the law of wisdom, you cannot dissociate the idea of wisdom from the foundation of gaining knowledge.

A dull ax requires great strength: be wise and sharpen the blade.

Ecclesiastes 10:10, TLB

That's the value of wisdom—it helps you succeed. The blade in this verse represents you and me. We sharpen the blade (ourselves) by gaining knowledge. Then wisdom comes to us from that knowledge. It's a progression. We start with building knowledge, and in turn, gain understanding. As we continue to walk in that understanding, we grow in wisdom. Yet, many Christians think if they just

CHAPTER SEVEN: GOD'S LAWS OF WEALTH

stand to the side and pray, God will deliver wisdom. Yes, He will deliver, but we have to work with Him, too.

If any of you lacks wisdom, let him ask of God, who gives to all liberally.

James 1:5

This verse tells us that God answers our prayers and will deliver wisdom. In times of decision making, it's wonderful to ask God to show you the right path. But this scripture does not exist as an excuse for laziness or lack of preparation. We shouldn't use this scripture out of context. We always need to be meeting God in the creative process. When we work toward His promises, He will deliver.

Wisdom begins with knowledge and understanding. After I've worked on the first two—knowledge and understanding—and established my foundation, I stand and ask for wisdom by implementing James 1:5.

And God gave Solomon wisdom and exceedingly great understanding, and largeness of heart like the sand on the seashore."

1 Kings 4:29

We all know Solomon's prayer, where instead of asking for wealth and riches, he said, "God instead of just giving me those things, I'm asking you to give me wisdom."

We often skim this verse and don't realize that Solomon applied these principles in his own life. Instead of removing the idea of wisdom from the idea of gaining knowledge, Solomon embraced it. He understood that he must apply himself to knowledge.

Just a couple of verses later in 1 Kings 4:33, the Bible says that Solomon described the plant life from the cedar of Lebanon to the hyssop that grows out of the walls. He learned about animals. He applied himself to gaining knowledge about birds, reptiles, mammals and fish. And then Solomon became the most successful exporter of his time. He made strong shields and raised powerful war horses. He was a brilliant businessman. That's why the Queen of Sheba came to see all of his wealth.

Solomon is a perfect example of how money is attracted—not pursued. By applying himself to knowledge and then asking for and walking in the wisdom of God, Solomon moved forward into a place of great wealth. Instead of asking for and receiving wealth and riches, wealth and riches were attracted to him because of the knowledge, understanding, and wisdom he obtained.

For several years, I worked with large companies that would sometimes invest in other companies. Whenever we were examining a company, one of the things we always looked for was who the principals in the company were. We wanted to know about their education, background, and experience.

In an investable company, we wanted to see how the people in leadership exemplified knowledge, understanding and wisdom in running their business. Bill Ackman, one of the largest hedge fund managers in America today, always bets on the horse. He invests in the people that are running companies and their ability to do that.

One of the secrets to Warren Buffet's success is that when he invests in companies, he moves to own the whole company outright. If Buffet thinks it's a good company, and the CEO or COO is not doing a proper job, he will buy the company under value. Then when he acquires the company, he will put in his own CEO or COO to run things in order to bring the value up.

And they will dash you down to the ground, you [Jerusalem] and your children within you; and they will not leave in you one stone upon another, [all] because you did not come progressively to recognize and know and understand [from observation and experience] the time . of your visitation [that is, when God was visiting you...] (emphasis mine)

Luke 19:44, AMP

Sometimes we have God-opportune moments in our lives, and we don't even recognize them. We don't recognize—progressively come to know and understand from observation and experience—that God is doing good things for us.

When I'm on the track of building the Second X and I understand the law of wisdom is a vital part of that process, I start with knowledge and move to understanding. Then I can graduate to walking in wisdom. That observation stage is knowledge, and experience is the understanding. Learn to apply yourself and experience things.

It's like how my grandsons play sports. I can play in the backyard with them all day long and help them develop some fundamental skills for baseball or soccer, but the challenge is that they're not going to learn unless they get in the game. You have to get your feet wet. You have to step into the water so the waters can part. If you don't progressively come to know and understand, you won't recognize the time of your visitation.

That's why, when we look at Genesis 1 and talk about being fruitful, we need to know how to be fruitful. In order to be fruitful, you've got to get in the game. You're never going to develop understanding unless you observe and experience, and you can't observe and experience unless you jump in the game.

Find places where you can get your feet wet. Find areas where you can serve or volunteer, or when it comes to building the Second X in business or real estate, find a mentor or take a class. Begin to take the steps you know to take in order to move in the direction you need to go. Regardless of how you do it, make sure you keep a careful catalog or journal of exactly what you learn along the way. This will prevent you from making the same fundamental mistakes in your future.

The Law of Wisdom is critical to being able to build the Second X. It's essential that you become a resilient learner. You've got to learn how to move forward. When things happen—instead of giving up and saying life doesn't work—be resilient. Pick yourself back up and try again. Take wisdom from your experience and the next time, try again a bit differently.

One of my mentors once told me that he had filed bankruptcy three times. Now, don't go filing bankruptcy three times if you can help it, but learn from his resilience. He picked himself back up from those low points and learned from his experiences. Eventually, he became a huge blessing to the kingdom of God—all because he was willing to keep trying!

Learn from your mistakes. Profit is made by solving problems that others cannot solve. Profit is also made by solving your own problems.

One of the things you learn in real estate investing, especially when buying multi-family units, is that there are complexes where all the utilities are not separately metered. When I was young, I purchased a simple property. It was a duplex, and I was convinced that all the utilities were separately metered. Well, I learned quickly that the three key words in real estate investing are verify, verify, verify, not location, location, location.

It turns out that the water meters were not separately metered, and one month I had to pay the water costs for that entire building. I had a water bill for $630 for one month! I didn't know you could even use that much water. It was a painful experience!

Within two months, I figured out the issue: there was a leak in one of the toilets. I immediately spent $1,500 to have the water metered for each unit. I spent $1,500, got the problem fixed, and picked myself back up. Now, any time I look at multi-family properties, I get on my hands and knees because I want to see working, individual water meters in the ground, and I want to see them before I purchase it!

That is what resilient learning looks like. It's painful sometimes, but it leads to great rewards and wisdom. Pick yourself up, pay your $630 water bill, and say, "Praise the Lord. Let's move forward!"

THE LAW OF CONNECTION

Then you say in your heart; 'My power and the might of my hand have gained me this wealth.' And you shall remember the Lord your God for it is He who gives you the power to get wealth, that He may establish His covenant which he swore to your Fathers, as it is this day.

Deuteronomy 8:17-18

God gives us the power to get wealth. But how does He do that? Well, we can read books and listen to teachings and above all, be a resilient learner. But here's my direct experience with this law of connection. I deeply believe in this law because it's something that has changed my life many times.

Felix Dennis was practicing the Third X when he said, "I was put on earth to get rich, to collect the money that already has my name on it, and then give it all away."

After Andrew Carnegie passed away, a card was found in his desk. On it, Carnegie had written, "I am going to spend the first half of my life accumulating money, and I am going to spend the last half of my life giving it all away." And that's exactly what he did! He gave all of it away. That's the Third X.

Building wealth should never be about becoming a Scrooge and hoarding; it should be about impacting the kingdom and changing the world for the better. The law of connection helps us build wealth. God gives us power to get wealth by offering us divine connections and Kairos moments.

> Since you were precious in My sight, you have been honored, and I have loved you; therefore I will give men for you, and people for your life. Fear not, for I am with you; I will bring your descendants from the east, and gather you from the west.

> Isaiah 43:4-5

God has people to help us on the path He wants us to go. These are people we might not even have met yet, but they will help us as we travel on our journey to build wealth. God has experiences for us that we've not yet had, which will empower us. When He brings these people and experiences across our paths, we call them divine connections.

My wife, Becky, and I have been married some 40 plus years. We were high school sweethearts, and for decades, every morning that we are physically together, we pray for our divine connections from the Lord. We pray like this: "Father, we thank You. You have people for our lives, and we believe there are people in the north. We believe there are people in the south. We believe there are people in the east. We believe there are people in the west. Lord, we speak to the north, we speak to the west, we speak to the east, we speak to the south and we command it to give up the people that belong in our lives." Then, as we come across people throughout our day, we believe that God has divine appointments that in many cases lead to divine connections.

On the day that I was born and my parents got my birth certificate, I believe that God set aside a treasure chest for me that was full of people and experiences for my future. And it's those people and experiences—those divine connections—that propel me to the place of going from the Second X to the Third X. They help me to impact the world with the gospel of Jesus Christ and the kingdom.

I believe God has a treasure chest like this set aside for everyone. But sadly, many people have never even tried to open the lid. How do you open your treasure chest? Well, that begins by praying every morning, "God, thank You for the divine connections You have planned for me. Help me to receive them." You pray and believe that for your life, and then you get your binoculars out and start looking for them. I'm not talking about taking advantage of people or practicing self-promotion, I'm talking about being sensitive to who God brings across your path. He always has a greater purpose for the people He puts in our path than we realize at the time.

I remember my first divine connection in the area of wealth building. When I met this particular man, wealth building was nowhere on my radar. I was in my early twenties, and at the time, I was just trying to pay my bills. It wasn't until a couple of years later that I realized how much I learned from this man. And to be frank, in the beginning I didn't even like him very much! But the more I listened to what he had to say, the more I realized that he knew some stuff that I didn't know. And it was good stuff!

Looking back, I don't believe there was anything he shared with me in the area of business that wasn't absolutely right on. Some of the foundational wisdom he poured into me was a divine connection. I didn't even realize that it was happening at the time. God used his wisdom to put me on the right path. I believe that God has people like this for your life too.

Decades ago, I was pastoring a church. I would preach on Sunday mornings, and we would sell cassette tapes (if you can remember what those are). If the tape department came up to me and told me that we sold five tapes on a Sunday morning, we thought we were having revival!

Every Sunday morning, we had a visitor packet that we would hand out, and in those packets, we would put one of my better recordings—either one called "The Seven Steps to Reaching Your Dreams" or "Five Characteristics of a Healthy Family." The visitors could choose which one they wanted. Then one day, while I was standing in a Ford dealership getting the oil changed in my red Ford Explorer, my phone rang. Back then, I had this huge cellphone—this was way before smart phones—that didn't have caller ID. So, when my phone rang, I answered it.

"Is this Pastor Billy Epperhart?"

"It is. How may I help you?" I was curious to know who the caller was because the only people who had my number were my wife and my secretary. Nobody else would call that number. So I knew if this guy was calling, then either my wife or my secretary had given my number to him, and that meant it must have been important.

He replied, "I have a cassette tape of yours. As a matter of fact, I have two cassette tapes of yours, and I've given them a listen. We want to publish these."

140

So there I was, waiting on my oil change, and this guy calls me out of the blue saying he wants to publish my cassette tapes. "Uh, huh," I said, "how does that work?"

"Just send me two tapes a month out of what you preach or speak on at church. We'll take a listen, clean out personal details related to your church, and duplicate it."

"How many tapes do you send out?" I said.

"Well, we send out about 35,000 tapes a week. You would get paid royalties per tape. You just send us the message, we produce everything, and then we will send you X amount per tape that is sold."

"So you send out 35,000 tapes a week, and you're going to pay me a royalty per each tape sold?"

"Yes! We'll send you a check once a month on the royalties."

I agreed to do this, and the royalty checks that came off of those cassette tapes replaced my total pastoral income at that time in my life—and then some. It was amazing!

So how did that happen? Well, a man and a woman whom I'd never seen before walked in the back door of my church one day. They were genuine visitors. They got the visitor packet, took the tapes home and listened to them. The woman liked the "Five Characteristics of a Healthy Family," and the man liked "The Seven Steps to Reaching Your Dreams."

They sent the tapes to his work on the east coast and from that little connection, I was able to more than double my income. The content on those tapes were teachings I gave to a Wednesday night group of 30 adults, but through that divine connection, God amplified it to 35,000 households!

It is so worthwhile to prayerfully begin taking the steps to obey God's plan for your life. When we talk about God giving us the power to get wealth, it doesn't mean that He's going to rain money down from heaven on you. It means He's going to give you the ability and connections to get wealth.

How does that happen? It happens through divine connections that God brings to us. He helps us to either learn how to do something or how to gain something. All of a sudden, this divine appointment will lead to a divine connection that actually shows us something we've never seen, heard or learned before. Start believing God to bring divine connections to you!

I've experienced times of drought in my life when it seemed like there were no divine connections happening, and I realized that I had to make a shift in what I was believing in my heart. Every day, my wife and I would get up and say, "If God be for us, who can be against us?" We would also say, "God has divine connections and kairos moments for our lives." Then we would quote Mark 11:23:

> **For assuredly, I say to you, whoever says to this mountain, 'Be removed and be cast into the sea,' and does not doubt in his heart, but believes that those things he says will be done, he will have whatever he says.**

> **Mark 11:23**

When you start practicing your faith and exercising your prayer life in these areas, God will begin to stir things up. Things will start happening. Movement will happen in the earth, and divine appointments will begin to come across your path.

Years after that phone call, I received another phone call, except this time it was from my office. I didn't physically come in to the office a whole lot at that time, but on that particular day, I came in.

Normally, my secretary would always knock on the door and wait before entering my office, but this day, she just marched in without knocking, looked at me, and said, "Pick up the phone."

"What?" I asked.

"Pick up the phone."

So despite being baffled, I picked up the phone. The man on the other end asked, "Is this Billy Epperhart?"

"It is. How may I help you?" I knew he must have told my secretary something interesting or she wouldn't have barged into my office like she did.

"You have a business on the east coast I'd like to buy," he said.

I had a bit of money in that particular business that he was interested in buying. It wasn't much, but we had grown, and things were happening.

"It's not for sale," I said.

He came back to me with a seven-figure cash offer. Cash! I have to admit, he got my attention.

"Well, do you have the money?" I asked. I mean, if someone tells you they're going to pay cash for your business, you at least need to ask that question. I wanted to know if he really had the money or was going to try to get me to finance it.

"I have the money. I want to pay you that amount, and I want to close in ten days."

"Well, you can't close in ten days. You've got to do your due diligence."

"I've already been doing my due diligence. Don't worry about it, if you're willing to sell it to me."

I was interested at this point. So I said, "Well, listen, I'm getting ready to go on a trip, so I'll be out of town for a while."

"I'm in town," he said.

"What?"

"I'm in town. I live southwest of Denver, and I'm staying in Lone Tree right now. I can meet you by the big fireplace at Nordstrom's in Park Meadows Mall."

What is one to do at that point? So I went over and met with him, and we talked. After I went home and talked with my wife and prayed about it, we decided to make the move. I sold him that business as it was, and we closed for seven figures—cash! And I tell you what, there is something powerful about being able to put that kind of money, in cash, without any liability spoken against it, into the bank in one event.

I had not even been praying to sell this business. But I had been praying and believing for divine connections. Then all of a sudden, God showed up and blessed me in the most awesome way. He had a divine connection for me!

THE LAW OF STEWARDSHIP

The law of stewardship is another important law of wealth. Implementing the law of stewardship is when we do our half, and God does His. This is about following all of the laws of wealth and bringing a level of intentionality into our finances. When we steward what God has given us, we master our money.

> Now it came to pass in the thirty-seventh year of the captivity of Jehoiachin king of Judah…that Evil-Merodach, king of Babylon, in the first year of his reign, lifted up the head of Jehoiachin king of Judah and brought him out of prison.
>
> Jeremiah 52:31 NKJV

The Amplified Bible even says that he "…lifted up the head of Jehoiachin king of Judah [and showed favor to him]." Favor was being released.

The New King James Version goes on to say in verses 32-34:

> He [the king of Babylon] spoke kindly to him [Jehoiachin] and gave him a more prominent seat than those of the kings who were with him in Babylon. So Jehoiachin changed from his prison garments, and he ate bread regularly before the king all the days of his life. And as for his provisions, there was a regular ration given him by the king of Babylon, a portion for each day until the day of his death, all the days of his life.
>
> Jeremiah 52:32-34 NKJV

So, Jehoiachin got released from prison. He got new clothes, a place to live, and a continual allowance all the days of his life. I like those kind of allowances! They are the asterisks in the Second X.

As I was reading through this passage once, I remember saying under my breath, "Lord, why did this happen? All the other kings were there, but you only elevated and favored Jehoiachin. You make it clear throughout Scripture that You are no respecter of persons. So why would You be a respecter to Jehoiachin and not the other kings? Why was he unique?"

After praying, I went back to study the meaning of Jehoiachin's name using a reference book called Hitchcock Bible Names. I looked up his name and found that it meant "preparation." It was a very common practice in ancient times to name people prophetically or to rename them in stories based on how they lived.

Jehoiachin was in prison for 37 years before he was lifted up and shown favor. And if his name meant "preparation," then I think it's safe to assume that during those 37 years, he was preparing. I believe he kept his heart in the right place and his mind active. I think that he never gave up, but continually prepared himself for the next step.

Jehoiachin was operating in this last law of wealth—the law of stewardship. He had a faith that did not waver. His heart, his mind, his mouth, and his body were all lining up for whatever God brought into his life. He was believing that something wonderful was in his future. I believe Jehoiachin was living as a steward in the middle of a seemingly never-ending desert. Then, all of a sudden, after many years, the king reached down and lifted him up above all of the other kings.

This is where the law of stewardship steps in. It positions us so to take the steps that we're supposed to take. It prepares us for whatever God has next. Now, this is not like winning the lottery. Because if you win a million dollars in the lottery, you better work hard to keep that money. So many lottery winners, whether they win a million or 500 million dollars, lose that money within five years. This is because they have no idea how to manage that kind of wealth.

Patience is the key to the law of stewardship. Jehoiachin had patience. He waited 37 years! That's a lifetime. By patience, I don't mean you just sit and wait forever. You exercise patience by conditioning your mind and staying prepared while you wait.

The stories of the Rothschild and Vanderbilt families are a great representation of the law of stewardship. Most people have heard of Cornelius Vanderbilt, but very few have heard of Amschel Rothschild. Vanderbilt died in 1877, and at the time of his death, he had amassed a fortune of $105,000,000. For his time, you could pretty much call him Bill Gates.

In 1972, 120 of Vanderbilt's heirs met in a hotel room in Nashville, Tennessee. In this meeting, they discovered not one millionaire existed in the entire group. Cornelius Vanderbilt had only left his money behind; he never taught them how to handle that kind of wealth.

The companies he set up worked, but the lack of training to his descendants was the ultimate downfall. Cornelius Vanderbilt's fortune ended up completely squandered by 1972. One-hundred years after his death, it was all gone!

Then there's Amschel Rothschild who lived in Frankfurt, Germany. He died in 1812. The Rothschild's are a banking family in Europe. Rothschild had five sons who moved to five different capitals in Europe. Amschel Rothschild gave his sons two options whenever they looked to start a business. He formed a family bank out of his fortune, and with that family bank, the sons could either: a) borrow the money and pay back the bank on terms, or b) allow the bank to take an equity position in their company and provide equity instead of debt.

He required his sons to study business. Then when they dove into a new business, they had to write everything they learned down and report it to the family bank. This way all of the heirs could share in that knowledge.

As of 2015, the Rothschild family still has an enormous fortune, and the reason they still have their fortune is because Amschel Rothschild understood the power of the law of stewardship. You have to teach people how to handle money, especially in such massive amounts.

I think the power of the law of stewardship is summed up in these two statements from the families: One of the Vanderbilt's grandsons who got to enjoy some of the wealth said, "Inherited wealth is a real handicap to happiness... It has left me with nothing to hope for, with nothing definite to seek or strive for."

One of Rothschild's grandsons, Nathan, said, "It requires a great deal of boldness and a great deal of caution to make a great fortune, and when you have got it, you require ten times as much wit to keep it."

How does the Bible handle the law of stewardship? A perfect example is Jesus' parable of the talents. In this parable found in Matthew 25:14-30, the master of a house comes and gives five talents to the first servant. This servant takes the five talents and makes five more so that he now has ten. When the master returns, he says, "Well done, good and faithful servant; you were faithful over a few things, I will make you ruler over many things."

Then he gives the second servant two talents. The servant takes these and makes two more, so that he has four. When the master returns, he says, "Well done, good and faithful servant; you were faithful over a few things, I will make you ruler over many things."

And finally, the master comes to the third servant and gives him one talent. This servant buries his talent in the ground. When the master returns, the servant runs to the field, digs up the talent and hands it back. The master becomes angry and says, "You wicked and lazy servant, you knew that I reap where I have not sown, and gather where I have not scattered seed. So you ought to have deposited my money with the bankers, and at my coming, I would have received back my own with interest."

And then something peculiar happens. The master takes that one talent from the third unfaithful servant and hands it to the first faithful servant who has ten talents. He says, "For to everyone who has, more will be given."

I used to always wonder why this happened. What was the master's point? And after prayer and study, I came to realize that it is because he was a faithful steward of his master's money. The reality is that money is attracted, not pursued.

When I properly operate in the Law of Stewardship and bring value to the marketplace, I become a faithful steward. Then the supernatural happens, and one gets added to ten. The divine connection comes along because I have been operating from a foundation of stewardship in my life. That's why in Deuteronomy 8:17, we read "And you shall remember the Lord your God for it is He who gives you the power to get wealth."

When we follow the law of stewardship in our lives, something supernatural happens. That one talent will be added to us, and then another and another. And that's where God gives us the power to get wealth.

 **SUMMARY**

When we partner with God in these laws, He gives us the power to get wealth.

The law of change: When there is new wine, we must offer God a new wineskin. With this new wineskin, we offer God a renewed mind. It means that we must have a spirit ready to change.

The law of wisdom: Too often we disassociate the idea of having wisdom from the idea of obtaining knowledge. We think wisdom just happens. But we need a foundation of knowledge for wisdom to grow upon.

The law of connection: God gives us the power to get wealth by offering us divine connections and kairos moments. God has people for our lives who will help us on the path He has for us. Every day, my wife and I get up and say, "If God be for us, who can be against us?" And we say, "God has divine connections and kairos moments for our lives."

The law of stewardship: Implementing the law of stewardship is when we do our half, and God does His. This is about following all of the laws of wealth and bringing a level of intentionality into our finances. When we steward what God has given us, we master our money.

PART THREE:

SERVING

CHAPTER EIGHT:

THE THIRD X, A BIG CHOICE

After all of this effort put into learning the recipe, finding the ingredients, and making the pancakes, you finally reach the moment when you can serve them. You set a plate of fluffy pancakes down before your wife, and watch her smile with surprise and delight.

Just like this metaphor, after you have put in the effort, mastered your money, and built wealth, you get to serve. Now you have wealth that can be directed any way you want it to be. You have reached the Third X.

Of course, you can give at every X. In fact, you should always be tithing and giving. You don't have to wait to serve, but you release a level of fully owning your options for giving at the Third X. Instead of taking your wife out to breakfast, you're able to fully own the process of making her breakfast. You have a deeper level of ownership and ability at the Third X.

The triangles start quite a bit out from where the Second X is formed. This is intentional. It shows you that you need some income. You must have the ability to live off of the Second X income. But at some point, once you have established a satisfactory lifestyle for yourself, you will start to really build wealth— above and beyond what you know to do with.

When you build this wealth, God blesses you so you can be a blessing to others. This is the moment where you get to fulfill the other half of the Abrahamic covenant. This is the moment where, through you, nations can be blessed.

> Get out of your country, from your family and from your
> father's house, to a land that I will show you. I will make
> you a great nation; I will bless you and make your name
> great; and you shall be a blessing I will bless those who
> bless you, and I will curse him who curses you; and in you
> all the families of the earth shall be blessed.

Genesis 12:1-3

At the Third X, you have become an investor who holds assets that yield much fruit to enjoy. Your money is working without you, and you have a big choice to make: Will you build bigger barns, or will you put your money to work for the kingdom?

PERFECTING MY PITCH

In 1974, I attended Oral Roberts University on a baseball scholarship. I was a pitcher, believe it or not. At the high school and college level back in the 70s, we played with wooden bats instead of metal ones, and let me tell you, hitting a ball with a wooden bat is a very different experience!

I headed to the university, thinking I was hot stuff. The first day we practiced, they put the other freshmen up to bat against me. I pitched my best fast ball three times in a row. On the third pitch, a freshman knocked the ball—with a wooden bat—in Tulsa humidity—410 feet over the centerfield wall! That was a pro-level shot! I immediately thought, "Toto, you ain't in Kansas anymore."

The pitching coach, a previous Dodgers pitcher by the name of Rich Calmus, came out to the mound after the hit and said, "Epperhart, we're going to have to give you another pitch." So he taught me how to throw a "slider." I learned the grip for a slider, and it dramatically helped me get people out at the plate.

We played our first game as a team against Oklahoma Baptist. I was put in to pitch at the beginning of the second inning, and the first three guys all hit shots on me. The bases were loaded in six to eight pitches. I was feeling the pressure at this point! Now, in high school, if that happened, the coach would have said, "Epperhart, throw the ball harder!" or "Throw more strikes!" None of these things would actually adjust anything however.

Rich Calmus walked out to the mound, came up to me and said, "Epperhart, let me see your slider." So I held up my grip. He didn't say a word. He just reached up, took my middle finger and moved it one eighth of an inch from the left side of the seam to the right side of the seam. Then without a word, he turned and walked off.

I struck out the next three batters! No one scored.

A ONE-EIGHTH INCH ADJUSTMENT

That one eighth of an inch adjustment made a dramatic difference in the effect I was able to have in that game and in future games. It's amazing how such a small shift can drastically change a result. I believe that we, as believers, also need to make an eighth-inch adjustment when it comes to our mindset as Christians. We need to adopt a kingdom mindset.

Believers of other religions can have a kingdom mindset. One time, a famous Christian evangelist preached a crusade in Nairobi, and thousands of people were saved. But then a religious group came in right behind him and offered microfinance loans to the new converts, so many converted to their religion.

While the Christian evangelist had a gospel of salvation mindset, which is essential, this group had a gospel of the kingdom mindset, and their kingdom gospel is what captured the hearts of those people. This is because faith without works is dead (James 2:20). I'm not saying that evangelist's faith was dead, but the way faith had been preached was, in some sense, dead. If after those people took the first step of accepting the Lord, the evangelist's group would have followed up with poverty-eliminating empowerment, those people might have truly understood and become a follower of Christ. But evangelism alone—without bringing the kingdom of God to earth—can fall flat.

Let's say you preach the gospel to a group of drug addicts and they accept Christ. Then you rejoice over them and leave them to their newfound freedom. Here's the problem: They have no consistent revelation of Christ's love in their lives. Consequently, they will turn around the next day, feeling the same addiction and loneliness as before because they don't know how to implement what you've given them.

The gospel of the kingdom is the second half of this tale. It's about going into a place and bringing Christ's peace into it—permanently. It's about transforming hearts, minds, and lifestyles. It's tikkun olam—elevating the poverty and sadness in the world to the holy.

I like to think of this in terms of Maslow's hierarchy of needs. Chances are that you are familiar with this graph, but we don't often think about it when it comes to our approach to missions.

Maslow's hierarchy of needs is interesting because it gives us an idea of how people work from the bottom up. The idea is that people have needs that should be met in a particular order. Therefore, if their primary needs are not being met, they won't fully understand having their secondary needs met.

According to Maslow, people's needs should be met in this order: physiological needs (breathing, food, sleep), then safety needs (security of employment, a home, health), then their need for love/

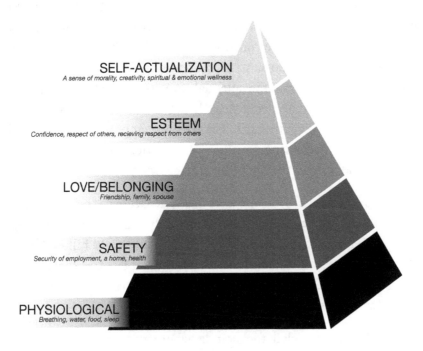

belonging (friendship, family, a spouse), followed by esteem (confidence, respect of others, receiving respect from others), and finally ending with self-actualization (a sense of morality, creativity, spiritual wellness).

Then Jesus went about all the cities and villages, teaching in their synagogues, preaching the gospel of the kingdom,

and healing every sickness and every disease among the people.

Matthew 9:35

Jesus was teaching and preaching, but notice that He was also ministering to the physical needs of the people. As followers of Christ, we should be mimicking His model. Physical needs and spiritual needs are important. It can never be one without the other. Until people experience the spiritual revelation of salvation through Jesus, they won't be prepared to understand that it is God who gives them the power to get wealth, but without empowering them with practical information and resources, their understanding of the kingdom of God will only scratch the surface.

Those people in Nairobi were ready to accept Christ, but they didn't know how to follow Him. They didn't know what the kingdom of God looked like. So before they could truly follow Christ, they needed to understand how to follow Christ. And that's where the gospel of the kingdom comes in. We need to meet their spiritual needs, as well as their basic needs.

In 2015, I traveled to Uganda where my non-profit, Tricord Global, had invested a $500,000 loan package to Glory Bank. The pastor who founded Glory Bank came up to me and said this:

> "Listen. Do you know what's happening to our churches in the southern half of Kampala? We have a lot of Christian churches popping up, but another religion is coming in and buying the land out from under the churches. Then they're evicting them. I've got two churches that have been evicted off the land where they hold church (in tents). I want to start giving them loans for their land. I'll help teach them to run their churches financially. Billy, if we do loans to those churches, then they can own their land and have pride of stewardship."

I thought to myself, Now, that's a kingdom mindset. It goes a step beyond just understanding the gospel. It involves strategic ways of empowering the kingdom of God to expand in a city or in a nation.

As Christians, we've got to start thinking differently. We need an eighth-inch adjustment. We need to continue preaching the gospel of salvation, but we need to add the gospel of the kingdom. And the gospel of the kingdom is about two things: the purpose of the church and nation transformation.

THE KINGDOM OF HEAVEN

And the disciples came and said to Him, 'Why do You speak to them in parables?' He answered and said to them, 'Because it has been given to you to know the mysteries of the Kingdom of Heaven, but to them it has not been given.'

Matthew 13:10-11

The phrase Jesus uses is the "kingdom of Heaven." In Matthew 6, Jesus prayed, "Your kingdom come, Your will be done, on earth as it is in heaven." So the kingdom of Heaven is in heaven. But the kingdom of God is really in the earth. When Jesus prayed Your kingdom come in the earth as it is in heaven, He was referring to the kingdom of God. He was saying that it was already established in heaven, and now He wants to establish it in the earth. Heaven has all of these problems answered: poverty, sickness, and drugs—but we need to answer those problems in the earth.

> But hear the parable of the sower: When anyone hears the word of the Kingdom, and does not understand it, then the wicked one comes and snatches away what was sown in his heart.
>
> Matthew 13:18

I'm convinced that the church has had a difficult time understanding the word of the kingdom. We have understood salvation, the Holy Spirit, faith, prayer, and, even for some, our identity in Christ. So when I'm talking about this, understand I'm only adjusting one eighth of an inch. We don't need to forget what's gone before, we just need to include the word of the kingdom. It's our job to infiltrate our society and culture with the kingdom of God. That's what the purpose of the church is.

> And I also say to you that you are Peter, and on this rock I will build My church, and the gates of Hades shall not prevail against it. And I will give you the keys of the Kingdom of Heaven, and whatever you bind on earth will be bound in heaven, and whatever you loose on earth will be loosed in heaven.
>
> Matthew 16:18-19

The Message Bible phrases it like this:

> And now I'm going to tell you who you are, really are. You are Peter, a rock. This is the rock on which I will put together my church, a church so expansive with energy that not even the gates of hell will be able to keep it out. And that's not all. You will have complete and free access to God's kingdom, keys to open any and every door: no more

barriers between heaven and earth, earth and heaven. A yes on earth is yes in heaven. A no on earth is no in heaven.

It's not about staying within the four walls of the church; it's about a kingdom message that penetrates every mountain of society all over the world—not just in the USA. It's about the gospel of the kingdom coming into the earth. The reason why the church has not taken up the causes on political and economic items at the level they should is because there is an isolation mentality instead of a kingdom mentality. There is a wind blowing for righteousness and for people getting involved in every area of society.

As long as we stay here, just in our church, the gates of hell will hold the mountains, but we've got to change our minds to begin to understand that it's not about the size of our church, it's about the condition of our city and our nation. The church has to start adopting a kingdom mindset.

ECCLESIA: A CITY COUNCIL

When we think about the kingdom of God, we need to understand the origin of the word *ecclesia*. Historically, we've said that it means "called-out ones," that we are called out from the world. But the word *ecclesia* came from Athens, Greece, and back then, it literally meant "an assembly." Specifically, it meant the public legislative assembly of the citizens of Athens. The Romans then adapted the word for the meaning of city council. A trumpet was blown, and the citizens would assemble. They would make a decision on the happenings in their city and nation by voting with a simple raising of hands.

For some reason, the church has this idea that we are called out from the world and that we're not supposed to go into the world.

And honestly? It's about the worst misinterpretation of the word you could ever have. When the Romans took some territory, they brought their government, merchants, businessmen, and politicians with them every place they conquered. Then they would tell the people of that place, "Listen. You can be with us or you can be against us. No problem. But if you're against us, we're going to kill your livestock and destroy your fields. Or you can be with us and join in with what we're doing. Then we can all grow and prosper together." They took their government everywhere they went.

> **For unto us a Child is born, unto us a Son is given; and the government will be upon His shoulder... Of the increase of His government and peace there will be no end.**
>
> Isaiah 9:6-7

We need to have an adjustment. Many times we've had nothing but a me gospel. But it's not only about you or me. It definitely includes you knowing who you are in Christ and understanding your authority in Christ, but you need an eighth-inch adjustment to understand that it's not about you building bigger barns for your own life. It's about city and nation transformation. It's about seeing families and lives changed all over the world. It's about the kingdom of God expanding in the earth. That's why Jesus prayed, "Your Kingdom come, Your will be done on earth as it is in heaven."

We, as the body of Christ, need to get a kingdom mindset. We need to understand that the church should really be the city council. It should be the legislative body coming into a kingdom. We should be so spread out across the Seven Mountains that we are the ones making the decisions for our cities and nations.

DISCIPLING THE NATIONS

Oral Roberts once said, "Whoever controls the finances of a city or nation will control the spiritual climate as well." It wasn't until I started going into third-world countries and investing money that I started thinking about how we as the church are holing up in a fortress, but it's really about city and nation transformation.

> **All authority has been given to Me in heaven and on earth. Go therefore and make disciples of all the nations, baptizing them in the name of the Father and of the Son and of the Holy Spirit, teaching them to observe all things that I have commanded you; and lo, I am with you always, even to the end of the age.**
>
> Matthew 28:18-20

We call this the Great Commission, and we often interpret it to mean "go and make disciples of the people in the nations." But what if it also means go and make disciples of the nations? The Bible says Jesus wept over Jerusalem not the people in Jerusalem. Of course, I fully believe that Jesus was weeping over the people, but it's not specifically the individuals.

We need to make an eighth-inch adjustment to think in terms of our cities and nations. When we understand this, we will start invading nations. We will look for the economy of the kingdom— the whole entirety of the kingdom of God. We will turn that nation into a disciple of Christ. What do you think other religions do?

Each disciple you make has the potential to grow in Christ, turn around, and start making other disciples. We disciple a nation when we disciple the people in that nation, but it can't just be about the 4 or 3,000 disciples you have. It has to be about the condition of that city and nation. Is that city or nation being transformed because of you?

> The Kingdom of God will be taken from you and given to a nation bearing the fruits of it.
>
> Matthew 21:43

What you do in a nation is critical.

> I must preach the Kingdom of God to the other cities also, because for this purpose I have been sent.
>
> Luke 4:43

THE CHURCH IN EVERY MOUNTAIN

We have thought that everything happens in the local church, yet it's about the domain of the King coming into our cities and nations. God does this in the end when the earth is renovated. The one thought that should occupy your endgame thinking is: How are you going to occupy the earth until He comes? That's what He's left us to do until Jesus returns. We are to do business and impact the cities and nations that we are in until He comes.

> Then Jesus went about all the cities and villages, teaching in their synagogues, preaching the gospel of the Kingdom, and healing every sickness and every disease among the people. But when He saw the multitudes, He was moved with compassion for them, because they were weary and

scattered, like sheep having no shepherd. Then He said to His disciples, "The harvest truly is plentiful, but the laborers are few. Therefore pray the Lord of the harvest to send out laborers into His harvest.

Matthew 9:35-38

Jesus instructed His disciples to go into the world and preach the gospel of the kingdom. If we are His disciples, we need to ask ourselves: "Are we really preaching the gospel of the kingdom? Are we really investing in city and nation transformation?"

Think about it. We had 300,000 people get saved in Nairobi, but we didn't continue practicing discipleship there. We all know how to raise money, but we don't have enough business sense to keep that money and use it well. This is why we have to be spread out across all Seven Mountains of society. The church should be in every mountain, and we should strive to be at the top of every mountain. Then we will have powerful influence in that culture. Adopting a kingdom mindset will change how you've been thinking about your career and influence.

There has been conflict between business and politics because the church could not embrace certain things. We had no context in which to put the content. The Seven Mountains simply give us a context. To operate in the kingdom, you have to know how to operate by faith. But Jesus didn't come just so I could be a big deal. He came so that I could have an impact on the world I live in. He came so that we could see the kingdoms of this world become the kingdoms of our God.

We let Satan have strongholds in our lives when we only think about ourselves instead of thinking about the bigger picture. There must be a bigger picture! The gospel of the kingdom is that bigger picture. Start praying for a revelation of what the bigger picture looks like in your own life. What mountain are you called to? How does God specifically plan for you to impact the city and nation you live in?

For me, that answer came through the business mountain. It came through building wealth and then using that wealth to start non-profits that change cities and nations. That's why you can tell I have a bent for the business world. I believe there is an alarm sounding right now that is calling Christians into the marketplace. That's why I teach and work in the marketplace. That's why I teach not just that you should do it but how to do it—and more importantly—how to do it from the kingdom perspective!

When you adopt a kingdom perspective, you can see that it's not just about you. Of course, God loves you and wants to have a relationship with you. But it's also about what God has called you to do and the expression of what God's called you to be. Go into all the Seven Mountains and possess them, in the name of Jesus!

DO BUSINESS UNTIL I COME

Then Paul spent two whole years in his own rented house, and received all who came to him, preaching the Kingdom of God and teaching the things which concern the Lord Jesus Christ with all confidence, no one forbidding him.

Acts 28:30-31

This is the last verse in Acts. When Paul was living in his rented house as a prisoner, he was teaching about Jesus.

We already know that we need to teach people the revelation of being born again. However, we tend to forget John 3:3, 5, where Jesus said:

> Most assuredly, I say to you, unless one is born again, he cannot see the Kingdom of God.... Most assuredly I say to you, unless one is born of water and the Spirit, he cannot enter the Kingdom of God.

Being born again is about entering a beautiful relationship with God, but we cannot disassociate a relationship with God from His kingdom. Relating to God is also about how we see and function in the kingdom. Paul was teaching on the kingdom of God and the Lord Jesus. We have to do both.

> But when they believed Philip as he preached the things concerning the Kingdom of God and the name of Jesus Christ, both men and women were baptized.
>
> Acts 8:12

These two go hand in hand—the gospel of salvation and the gospel of the kingdom.

The truth is that our lives should be about occupying until Jesus comes.

> So he called ten of his servants, delivered to them ten minas, and said to them, 'Do business till I come.'"
>
> Luke 19:13

We are to do business until Jesus comes back for His kingdom.

One of my pet peeves is that the church, in general, has not had a revelation of the kingdom. We need an eighth-inch adjustment. You don't have to change your eschatology, unless your eschatology is leading you to not occupy until He comes. I'm not trying to change your whole worldview, I just want to help you understand the part you play. Just an eighth of an inch.

> **The seventh angel then blew [his] trumpet, and there were mighty voices in heaven, shouting, The dominion (kingdom, sovereignty, rule) of the world has now come into the possession and become the kingdom of our Lord and of His Christ (the Messiah), and He shall reign forever and ever (for the eternities of the eternities).**
>
> Revelation 11:15, AMP

It's God's business to decide when, where, and how He returns. It's our business to occupy until He comes and to spread the gospel of salvation and the gospel of the kingdom. What are you and your church doing right now to have an impact on the kingdom? What kind of context are you putting what you believe in?

We have to continue to hear and read and speak the Word of God. Becky and I practice this every morning. After decades of following God, we realized it's not about us. We thank God that He takes care of us and our family, but it's about a lot more than that. It's about the kingdom and the kind of impact we are having on it. We need to start praying that the kingdoms of this world become the kingdoms of our God.

At the writing of this book, Charis Bible College has a business school, a media school, a political school, a ministry school, a missions school, a worship arts school, and a healing school. I can't say that they've intentionally aimed toward the Seven Mountains, but here they are training people to infiltrate all six mountains—all the while being the seventh: education.

All I know is that Andrew Wommack, the founder of Charis Bible College, prays and obeys. Charis is one of the only places in the world that you can go and get a seven-mountain training. It's time for us, as believers, to get a revelation and an eighth-inch adjustment on the kingdom of God in our lives. Jesus came preaching the gospel of the kingdom. We should just follow His example.

GOD NEEDS BUSINESSMEN TOO

R.G. LeTourneau, called God's Businessman by his peers, was a Christian businessman and entrepreneur. He was a true example of a kingdom-minded entrepreneur living in the Third X.

LeTourneau was brilliant but a bit eccentric. He worked in construction and earth moving, and was constantly underbidding his competitors to get jobs. But instead of living in the mold of his time, he invented machinery to help him get the job done even quicker. He eventually started his own business and worked as a manufacturer for Caterpillar—one of Warren Buffet's favorite stocks.

During the Great Depression, LeTourneau's business boomed. He became an incredibly wealthy man, but he never built bigger barns for himself. Instead, he and his wife, Evelyn, decided to give back to the kingdom. LeTourneau's designs are still being used today, yet he never finished high school. He just followed God's plan for his life, experienced divine connections, and practiced the law of wisdom.

The freedom that comes with the Third X is that you get to move from living off of 70 percent of your income to flipping that ratio entirely. You can live off of 30 percent and give and invest the other 70 percent! You don't need your money to live; therefore, you will have the freedom to build up the kingdom and impact your city and your nation.

By the end of his life, LeTourneau was giving away 90 percent and living off of 10 percent. That's what enabled him to give millions to Christian causes. But before he could reach this point, LeTourneau had to learn a lesson that we must learn. Like so many people today, he thought that the only way he could work for God was as a pastor or a missionary, yet here God had blessed him with the ability to invent industry-altering machinery.

LeTourneau brought the issue to his pastor, and that pastor changed his life in four words: "God needs businessmen too." And his pastor was absolutely right! God needs businessmen. And artists. And politicians. And musicians. And counselors. And engineers. And doctors. And pastors. God needs us in all areas of the Seven Mountains. God needs Christians who have wealth so we can impact the kingdom through empowering causes. If we are all pastors and missionaries, who will send us?

THE THIRD X AND THE LAW OF STEWARDSHIP

The big way I went about living out the Third X in my life was by starting Tricord Global. Our vision statement, "Transforming the world, one village at a time," is done primarily through microfinance. Tricord does other charitable work, such as drilling water wells, but I believe that microfinance loans to individuals and to banks are what will truly move people out of poverty.

In February 2015, we started a $500,000 investment going to the microfinance lending in Uganda. I combined all my years of knowledge and experience of using my own capital in order to be able to live at The Third X, so I could teach others how to live at the Third X. So now, not only do I get to give, but I also have an opportunity to help others give.

Your side of the fence is getting yourself in position to function in the Third X where you will have enough passive income coming off the asterisks that everything you need in your life will be paid for. Once your Second X income is taking care of you, your family, and your children, you will be able to create this Third X. At this point, you can choose to build bigger barns or to give it all away.

Many times, as we're giving on our side of the fence, we're not practicing the law of stewardship. Our purpose in making microfinance loans is not to try to make money. We do these microfinance loans because we are practicing the law of stewardship.

What has happened, in many cases in third world nations, like Malawi however, is that we have created a welfare mentality. We've been throwing fish to the people without teaching them the skills needed to help them maintain that lifestyle. In other words, we have just been throwing money at a wall to see if it sticks, instead of teaching people how to work and live.

We want people to fend for themselves, but when all the food is gone, where do they find more food? The idea behind the microfinance loan is that we take a dollar, and that same dollar is lent over and over. If we teach them how to fish and lend that dollar to them to get them started, then we're able to keep that dollar in the country through the interest rate that is charged. This enables us to continue with the process and help many more people. In our giving, we must think in terms of the law of stewardship in order to create sustainable enterprises in developing nations and at home.

THE BIG QUESTION

Using the story of LeTourneau, it's imperative that we begin to think in terms of kingdom enterprises that have a triple bottom line. The Triple Bottom Line (TBL) stands for three pillars: People, Planet, and Profit. But I have always preferred to think of it as: People, Purpose, and Profit.

The People: It's is all about discipling. It's giving people a hand-up instead of a handout. It's teaching them how to fish, and empowering them with knowledge and resources.

The Purpose: is the kingdom of God. It's working to see the kingdom of God established in the earth in all Seven Mountains, in all of the nations.

The Profit: We make a financial profit so we can lend the same dollar over and over again. In a lot of Christian missions, we give a dollar, but once that dollar is gone, we have to go back to western nations and raise another dollar. It's not that it's a bad thing to donate to causes; it's actually a wonderful thing. But at the Third X, we should be donating and investing. In TBL (Triple Bottom Line) thinking, we're able to raise investment dollars, and through proper use of the law of stewardship, we are able to keep that dollar in that country and use it over and over again.

Please don't misunderstand what I'm saying. I believe in philanthropy and giving, and that should always be at the forefront of our minds. But we have to make an eighth of an inch adjustment in order for us to add a sustainability mindset to our approach in third-world countries. To put it simply, the TBL approach is the approach that keeps on giving.

To build a kingdom wealth builder mindset and move forward from where you are today, you must first identify which X you are living in. Are you at the First, Second, or Third X? I've given you steps in this book, outlining what to do at each X in order to master your money. If you find yourself at the Second or Third X, then instead of building bigger barns, I encourage you to give to causes that are impacting cities and nations for the kingdom of God, and on top of that, I encourage you to invest some of your assets into causes that are impacting people for the kingdom with a profit.

It's an eighth of an inch adjustment. Keep on preaching the gospel of salvation but instead of leaving it there, go forward into preaching the gospel of the kingdom. Invade the Seven Mountains! Find which mountain God wants you to work in, and then put your all into that. Amplify your heart for giving with a heart for sustainable giving.

Money mastery is all about freedom. The question is, what will you do with that freedom? Will you build bigger barns or will you put your wealth to work for the kingdom?

SUMMARY

At the Third X, you have become an investor who holds assets that yield much fruit to enjoy. Your money is working without you, and you have a big choice: Will you build bigger barns or will you put your money to work for the kingdom?

We as believers need to make an eighth-inch adjustment when it comes to our mindset as Christians. We need to adopt a kingdom mindset.

As followers of Christ, we should be mimicking His model! Physical needs and spiritual needs are important. It can never be one without the other. Until the spiritual revelation of salvation through Jesus happens, they won't be prepared to understand that it is God who gives them the power to get wealth. But without empowering them with practical information and resources, their understanding of the kingdom of God will only scratch the surface.

It's not about staying within the four walls of the church. It's about a kingdom message that penetrates every mountain of society all over the world—not just in the USA. It is about the gospel of the kingdom coming into the earth.

We need to understand that the church should really be the city council. It should be the legislative body coming into a kingdom. We should be so spread out across the Seven Mountains that we are the ones making decisions for our cities and nations.

Oral Roberts said, "Whoever controls the finances of a city or nation will control the spiritual climate as well." It wasn't until I started going into third world countries and investing money there that I started thinking about how we as the church are holing up in a fortress, but it's really about city and nation transformation.

So being born again is about entering a beautiful relationship with God. But, we cannot disassociate a relationship with God from his kingdom. Relating to God is also about how we see and function in the kingdom.

In our giving, we must be thinking in terms of the law of stewardship in order to create sustainable enterprises in developing nations and at home.

Money mastery is all about freedom. The question is, what will you do with that freedom? Will you build bigger barns? Or will you put your wealth to work for the kingdom?

APPENDIX

CHECKLIST

Product or Service:

☐ What need am I filling?

☐ What problem am I solving?

☐ What can I do better?

☐ What is my business idea?

Guide Map:

☐ Written Business Plan

☐ Identify Competency Gaps

☐ Develop a Team (Connections)

Legal Beginnings:

☐ Determine Legal Structure (Sub S, LLC, LP)

☐ Register Name

☐ Get Tax ID Number

Financial Beginnings:

☐ Initial Funding

☐ Identify Income Sources

- ☐ Primary Cost Structures

- ☐ Bookkeeping

- ☐ Taxes

Marketing:

- ☐ Core Customers

- ☐ Channels

- ☐ Social Media

Key Systems:

- ☐ Office Operations

- ☐ Product or Service Development

- ☐ Inventory Control

- ☐ Order Processing/POS

- ☐ Accounts Receivable

- ☐ Customer Service

- ☐ Accounts Payable

- ☐ Marketing

- ☐ Human Resources

- ☐ Legal

- ☐ Real Estate

21 QUESTIONS TO GET YOU STARTED

No matter how small your idea is, you can never start testing the waters too early with a business model. Using the Business Model Canvas will help. You need to be thinking about whether you want to do business, invention or non-profit. You also want to immediately ask yourself the big questions: "Can it scale up?" (Which just means, for example if you're starting in Florida, can you eventually add operating in Seattle? Will it grow?), and "Can it be automated?" The key is this: Is your idea scalable?

But there is a lot more that goes into developing a business model. You need to learn to ask and answer the right questions.

Here are 21 Key Questions to help you get started developing your business plan:

1. What problem are you solving?

2. Is there a true need? Or will you need to differentiate yourself?

3. Why is the problem important?

4. What is your solution?

5. Describe your product or service in two or three sentences. Put it in terms anybody could understand—no techno speech!

6. What is your value proposition?

7. Why is your value proposition important to the customer?

8. Is your value proposition a nice-to-have or a need-to-have?

9. Who are your competitors? Name 3-5 competitors.

10. What do your competitors sell, and how does it compete against you?

11. How do you differentiate your product?

12. Draw a matrix that matches your product or service to your competitors.

13. Describe how your product or service differs from the competitors. (Price is not a good differentiator by itself!)

14. How large is this market? Define and size the market. (Make sure you focus on the addressable market.)

15. Who is your target customer? Provide a fairly detailed description of the target customer. Your business can be maybe a B2B or B2C.

16. What is your go-to market strategy and pricing model?

17. How do you intend to market your product or service?

18. Describe your pricing model.

19. What does your organization look like? Develop an Org Chart that represents your staffing at the end of the first full year of operation.

20. Who will be the King?

21. Write a 3-year financial projection. Keep it simple but well thought-out.

- Revenue (if more than one source, list it)

- Expenses (think about what you need to run the company)

- Gross Profit (how much will you make before interest, taxes and depreciation?)

CREDIT SCORE

FICO is the primary credit scoring agency in the U.S. It stands for Fair Isaac and Company. They are the company that actually designed the model for credit scoring.

FICO's model for creating a credit score is proprietary information and not made public. As long as I've been doing this, I've never come across information on the exact way FICO comes up with someone's credit score. A credit score in the U.S. determines how credit worthy a person is.

For example if you want to buy a home, whether or not you want to buy a personal home or invest in real estate, the first four loans of a year will be based primarily on your credit score. Besides a few other requirements that they have in the loan process, like income and other debts, credit score is the main thing. It tells the lender in simple terms how credit worthy you are.

For many people, keeping a close eye on their credit score and actively maintaining a healthy score can be a daunting task. This is especially true for anyone along the spectrum of new life choices or unexpected changes. Whether it's purchasing a vehicle or home, or perhaps a sudden barrage of medical bills, one can be faced with the reality of the power held by those three numbers.

Your credit score is composed of five determining factors: Payment History, Outstanding Credit Balances, Length of Credit History, Type of Credit and Credit Inquiries.

1. Payment History. Payment history is of very high importance as it accounts for 35% of your overall score.

Outstanding Credit Balance. Followed closely is your outstanding credit balance, which holds 30% of your score. It is important to maintain a good payment history and to monitor your Outstanding

Credit Balances closely. These have the greatest impact on your score and can affect it quickly. If you see a mistake in either of these areas, it is imperative to resolve it quickly for the sake of your score.

2. Length of Credit History. Over time, credit can improve with the Length of Credit History element, which accounts for 15%.

3. Type of Credit. This comprises 10% of your score.

4. Credit Inquiries. The final 10% of your credit score is made up by credit inquiries.

Unfortunately, about 79% of all credit reports contain mistakes of some kind. Furthermore, 25% of credit reports contain errors that result in credit denial. You should also frequently inspect your report for personal information, making sure what is listed is current and accurate.

Another important aspect to note on your report is the accuracy of your closed and open accounts. As many as 30% of reports incorrectly list closed accounts as open–which can negatively impact your score! To view your credit report and score, pay for a copy from each of the following agencies: *Experian, TransUnion and Equifax.* Most of the free reports don't include your credit score. And remember, lenders will use your middle score from each of the reporting agencies.

Monitor your credit closely and file any disputes promptly. If you work on improving the health of your credit score, you will benefit by receiving lower interest rates for future projects.

Defining the Score. Let's break down those numbers to get a better understanding of where you are and what it means for you.

- 850 = Highest. If you are here, you are golden. You can expect the lowest of interest rates. Any institution would be pleased to grant you a loan or anything else you might be requesting.

• 720 = Outstanding. This is an excellent score, and you can negotiate some good interest rates. Most institutions will grant approval with this score.

• 680 = Good. This is a decent score. You are looking at a little bit higher interest rates with the possibility of some hesitancy or possibly denial of larger loan amounts.

• 620 = Danger. This will cause concern for many institutions and higher interest rates.

• 500 = Needs Work. It will be difficult to get approval for loans and other financial endeavors. There are most likely red flags on your credit report that need your attention and action to resolve.

Keep your credit card balances no more than 50% of available credit! But really, the best case is to keep your balance no more than 33% of whatever your available credit is. So if you have a $10k limit, it's best not to owe more than $3,300 at any given time.

As an investor, **refi's are important to keep your money working.** You want to buy the property on 60-80 cents on the dollar, and you want to have paid 3 months of mortgage payments. Once you refinance, you want to make about 90 days of payments before you try to refi another property or a group of properties. So allow 3 months of mortgage payments to be made before refinancing another property.

In this process, you bring your credit score back up. Every time you refinance, especially if you refi several properties at a time, your credit score can take a 20-point hit—even if you're doing everything right! So allow that three months, and those 20 points will come back up. And then you can refi again.

Here's a real nugget: **Form a corporation, and have your autos and lines of credit put in the corporation's name.** Then be clear when getting loans that you do not want them reported on your personal credit at *all*.

I actually have no personal guarantees signed on the loans with any automobile company. The national credit company with that auto manufacturer has made me the loans strictly in my corporation's name. I have done business with them for a long enough time that we've established this trust. What does all that mean? I do not owe *anything* against myself on anything with this automobile company.

You can also do lines of credit in a corporation's name after you've established your reputation. And then I just always ask them to not report these things on my personal credit report because I do not personally own the money. Yes, I own the company. But the company as an entity acts as a third-person. And therefore you are able to take out loans, and it doesn't show up on your credit reports.

CREDIT SCORE DISPUTE PROCESS

Something to be wary of is the fact that 25 percent of credit reports contain errors resulting in credit denial. Therefore, it is important that you monitor your credit report and actually see what is on it. Years ago, there was an unpaid balance on my credit report that was way overdue. I never looked at my credit reports when I was younger, and it turned out that the debt wasn't even mine. I had no idea who the person was. Somehow it got on my credit report. A friend, who was a banker, pointed the overdue balance out to me, and I said to him, "Well, Bob, that's not mine." I knew nothing about it in those days, but he helped me work it out. We went through the dispute process and got everything straightened out.

An alarming 79 percent of all credit reports have mistakes of some kind. It could be anything from your name being misspelled to the wrong address. Also, 54 percent of credit reports contain incorrect personal information. For example, 30 percent had closed accounts listed as open.

Credit score is important at the first X because we need to get in position to receive wealth. Being empowered with the information to understand your credit report is important.

When you're disputing errors on a credit score, you can mail in the dispute. That takes about 30 to 45 days. You can also dispute errors online. And I highly recommend doing that as they can usually be resolved within 30 days.

If you have been denied credit many times, you can get things corrected in 24 to 48 hours. Lenders can actually do a "quick score" or a "rapid report" to get your credit score re-scored. This allows you to get credit.

DIVIDEND-PAYING STOCKS

Wise investors and those who wish to count on their wealth increasing have always and will continue to look to dividend stocks. The definition of a dividend-paying stock by www.investopedia.com is: "A dividend is a distribution of a portion of a company's earnings, decided by the board of directors, to a class of its shareholders. Dividends can be issued as cash payments, as shares of stock or other property." In this book we are emphasizing cash dividend payments instead of shares or other property paid to the stockholder.

Before the days of electronic trading, paper stock certificates were issued and were held by the owner at their home or place of business. If the owner of the stock desired to sell it, he had to take the certificates to a stockbroker who would issue a sell order and a new buyer would purchase them. Compared to today's market execution, it was an excruciatingly slow process. Today trades happen in milliseconds from the confines of someone's home office. We live in a different world. However, the fundamentals around what constitute a good investment are the same.

In order to gain some perspective, it helps to know that in the early part of the 20th century the only reason stocks were purchased was for the dividend that they paid. Then the roaring twenties came, and even though dividends were still paid, people speculated in stocks by counting on the underlying price of the stock to increase. Much like today. We know how that ended. The Great Depression happened.

Likewise the 1980s and 1990s experienced high capital growth of stocks once again. And the focus moved from dividends to growth. When stocks are increasing in value by 20 percent annually (1980s and 1990s), then a 7% dividend payout seems paltry. So most investors of this generation don't even think in terms of what kind of dividend a stock pays. However, going back in history, most stocks paid a dividend so someone could easily evaluate if a stock was a good investment for them by just looking at how much the dividend was.

Now let's be clear. A lot of money can be made in trading stocks. But a lot of money can also be lost trading in stocks. Warren Buffett says the secret to making money is NOT LOSING MONEY. A dividend-paying stock typically is very low risk and the dividend payout is mostly assured.

Companies that pay a dividend today mostly do it on a quarterly basis. To help you understand what kind of dividends are being paid today, I have included the chart below.

REASONS TO CONSIDER DIVIDEND-PAYING STOCKS

Dividend-paying stocks not only provide you with a recurring stream of income, but they also offer room for growth. This is critically important as your portfolio needs to keep pace with inflation in order for you to maintain the style of living to which you're accustomed. So below I have listed several benefits of dividend-paying stocks.

Better Income/Return than Bonds and CDs

U.S. Treasury securities or money market funds are paying such low rates that investors are looking to other places to meet their needs. Dividend-paying stocks can serve as a complement to other income investments in order to provide a steady source of income to yield-hungry investors. It should be noted that unlike the interest income paid on most bonds, dividend payments on stocks are at the sole discretion of the company and are subject to change. However, the investor can look at the last 5-10 years of dividends and closely ascertain what the dividend payment will be.

Tax Advantaged Income

The current dividend and capital gains tax treatment was established with the American Taxpayer Relief Act of 2012 (ATRA). You will need to check with your accountant to learn the specific advantage that you may enjoy. For most investors, the income will be treated at passive income rates or lower. Always check with your account or tax attorney to confirm the tax advantages for your situation.

Protection Against Inflation

Historically, owning stocks that regularly increase their dividend has proven to be a good hedge against inflation, especially compared to many bonds, which offer a fixed income stream over the life of the bond. In an inflationary environment, holders of fixed income securities can face sharp losses in the value of their bonds because the interest payments are not growing in a period where prices are escalating. Therefore, the bond income's purchasing power may decrease over time. While there is no guarantee that companies will continue to maintain or increase their dividends, if a stock's dividend does grow at a rate equal to or faster than inflation, the loss of purchasing power can be prevented.

Hedge Against Stock Market Volatility

Dividend-paying stocks have historically provided some downside protection in volatile market environments. Dividend-paying stocks are typically companies that have a historical record of generating strong earnings and cash flow, which gives them the financial strength to pay a dividend. As an investor, you should desire the stability of companies with a solid business model while seeking to manage risk in a declining market. Plus you still receive an income stream during a volatile market.

Potential Enhanced Total Return over Non-dividend Paying Stocks

As mentioned previously, dividends have historically represented a large portion of investors' total return. While that contribution waned in the 1980s and 1990s, in the period from 2000-2010, dividends provided a source of positive return as equity prices declined in this decade. As we rotate into the mid-2010s, continued favorable tax treatment and investors' increasing desire for income is influencing companies to place more emphasis on paying and raising their dividends.

As the baby boom generation matures, many of these investors entering retirement are faced with inadequate savings to fund their retirement, particularly given the sub-par yields (2015) being offered in the bond market. More of the baby boom generation shifting into retirement will increase demand for dividend-paying stocks over time.

Examples of Dividend-paying Stocks

Here are some stocks that anyone can add to their portfolio that pay handsome dividends while at the same time are enjoying capital growth. So remember that well-selected dividend-paying stocks not only pay consistent dividends, they can also experience increase in their stock price just like stocks that pay no dividend.

The fi rst we kn ow as th e "g olden ar ches." I sa w my fir st **McDonald's (MCD)** in 1967 in Killeen, Texas. I was from a small town in south Texas, and Killeen was a large city to me. On the sign it said something like "over 3 million hamburgers sold." Today, they have sold over 300 billion. Now that's growth! They say that they sell 75 hamburgers per second, 24 hours a day around the world.

Although we live in a day when everyone is much more health conscious about the food they eat, McDonald's is still selling plenty of hamburgers and fries. But they have also changed their menu to keep up the changing times.

Why do I like McDonald's as a core retirement stock? It's all about the dividend. McDonald's has raised its dividend every year since 1977, and its dividend has been increasing at a scorching pace over the past decade. McDonald's is a champion among retirement stocks, and you can buy it today with a 3.5% dividend yield.

One of Warren Buffett's favorite stocks is Coca Cola. Of course, Buffet likes dividend-paying stocks. **Coca Cola (KO)** was founded in 1892, has being paying quarterly dividends since 1920 and has increased dividends in each of the last 50 years. Wow! Now that represents consistency and strength. It is currently paying a 3.3% annual dividend.

Another dividend-paying stock that is listed as a Buffet favorite is **Procter and Gamble (PG).** According to Wharton School of

Business Professor, Jeremy Siegel, P&G would've turned a $10,000 investment in 1957 into more than $4 million today. Not bad for an "unexciting" asset in my opinion. In fact, this is proof that a stock can pay a dividend and still enjoy capital appreciation. What's more, even after 55 years of consecutive dividend increases for its shareholders, P&G still expects to increase its dividend 10% per year going forward. It is currently paying a 3.3% annual yield.

I thought I would throw in a stock that is not typically considered a dividend-paying stock, but it is. It has experienced an incredible increase in stock price value since its inception. **Intel (INTC)** has increased its dividend payout over the past five years by 26%. Its dividend-adjusted share price has grown by 16% on an annualized basis over the past 20 years—far superior to the adjusted returns of the S&P 500.

NEGOTIATION AND DOWN PAYMENT

When it comes to real estate investing, it is much more efficient if you have some of your own money. The power to negotiate with someone when you are purchasing a property is much greater when they know you actually have the money to buy it. You don't have to spend all your time finding creative financing. Instead, you just go in, make the offer and negotiate on value. I call it value investing in real estate. You negotiate and try to get the best price you can for the property.

You make money when you buy. In real estate, you make money when you buy—not when you sell. Not understanding that is one of the biggest mistakes real estate investors make. You always want to buy a property at a lower cost than what it's worth. I'm convinced of that. I've done real estate a couple of different ways, like where I've bought on terms instead of price.

But I can tell you from experience that the safest and best way to grow your investment is to buy your property with cash from a loan. This is why it's so important to understand real estate finance and to understand how to keep the money you have moving. You should also develop relationships with a mortgage banker and a mortgage broker.

80 cents on the dollar. It's therefore important to understand how to come up with a down payment. I always want to buy real estate at 80 cents on the dollar. In some cases, I'll purchase property at 60 or 70 cents on the dollar. But the safest place to be is no more than 80. To clarify, that's 80% of the real value of the property—even after repairs. When you're at 80%, this means you have 20% equity going into that property. So you're in pretty good shape if a little later you want to re-finance or even if you just want to hold it and pay it down. Regardless, you're still in good shape.

Down payment. What's important here is that you have to do a purchase mortgage. And on the purchase mortgage, you'll have to have a down payment. What I recommend is that you buy a prop-erty with 10% down. In some cases you can do it with 5%. I know investors who do it all the time. And if you have a really strong credit score there is actually 100% financing available.

In a 100% case, they typically will do what's called a 70-30 loan or a 70-25. That means for the first mortgage they'll loan you 75% of the purchase price of the property, and then you'll get a second mortgage at typically a much higher interest rate that is for 25%. You literally have a 100% on the loan. But be aware that you will still have to have some money for closing costs.

Negotiate with power. The point I want to make to you is that you are in a whole lot stronger position negotiating and personally if you actually are able to bring a little money to the table. Most lenders will want to see that you have six months of cash reserves of the mortgage payment—principal interest, taxes and insurance. They like to see that liquid in the bank. So if your mortgage payment is $1,000 a month, they like to see $6,000 liquid in the bank plus whatever the down payment is you've arranged. For example, on a $100k house you would need $10,000 for your down payment plus $6,000 in reserve.

Two simple ways to raise a down payment are through Liquid Assets (Cash, Stocks, Bonds, Insurance) and your Relatives/ Friends. But if that's not an option for you, check out these other ways:

☐ **Home equity (Refi/HELOC):** One of the greatest stagnant assets in America is home equity. As you learn how to invest in real estate, you'll realize that this is not a risk. You can pull money from the equity you have in your home by doing a cash out refinance loan, where you actually cash out your house. You do this by getting an appraisal of the new value of the home. Because it's appreciated over time and you have that equity in there, you can have the bank loan you 80-90% on the new value of your home. Then you can take that money and invest it in real estate. When I do seminars, I often hear people say that they won't cash out their equity because they want it. So often, I see people putting their equity on a credit loan where they go out and buy a huge TV. The problem is that this TV is worth a third of what they paid for it the moment they leave the store. Instead, you should put the money into an asset that will *appreciate* in value. The risk is much less! I strongly support using home equity to help you get started in real estate.

☐ **Retirement Accounts (IRA):** A lot of people don't know this, but you can now use your IRA to purchase a second home or to buy an investment property. The property needs to be in your retirement accounts. Typically the property would be tied on the trustee of the plan. Mortgage companies are okay with this. You can literally go get a mortgage on the property using your IRA to make the down payment and to make the monthly mortgage payments. Just remember that the payments must be made on the plan. You can also just borrow against your plan if that suits you better. And I don't think a lot of people realize that.

☐ **Lines of Credit (Local Banks):** With a true line of credit, you can write a check for anything you want—buy a pair of shoes or buy a house. I use lines of credit that way—**not** on my actual credit card though. Quite often, I have used lines of credit for rehabbing properties, and the property is not connected to the line of credit. The secondary line of credit is where the property *is* connected to what you're borrowing. For example: A while back, the bank I was with said I can be out buying properties up to a million dollars. For single-family homes, that really gives you an advantage on going in and buying the property! The bank has already given you the pre-approval letter.

☐ However, the bank will have certain ratios. Typically, a bank will not loan more than 80% of the appraised value of the house, and that includes rehab. So what that means is this: If you pay 70 cents on the dollar for the property, the bank would loan you 100% of the 70%. And then if you were going to use the ten cents on the dollar, they would loan you that extra ten percent to do the rehab.

☐ Some banks don't require you to put any of your money in that deal. There is tremendous leverage to go in and buy a property. Don't be concerned about talking to a hundred banks. Some banks simply don't work this way. It might not be in their lending portfolio. Instead, look for local banks who are more aggressive and who loan to builders, other investors, etc. Ask your attorney, your CPA or your real estate agents.

☐ You can get lines of credit that are connected to the property itself, and that gives you tremendous leverage in acquiring property. Most of those loans last for 6-12 months. I'll get mine for 12 months, and then I will refinance that loan when it starts coming out in 12 months. And in some cases because there's no seasoning requirement by local banks, you literally can refinance that loan in 60 days, get 100% of your money back and put that money in your pocket. Banks have no problem with this because they're loaning against an appraised value.

☐ **Credit Cards (Cash Advances):** Now to be completely honest, I'm not a big fan of this method. But I know investors I trust who have really made this plan work! That said, I would only recommend this if you really understand how to invest in real estate. Personally, I prefer to build relationships with local banks. And if you say your credit is not any good, I say go sit down with a local bank. They're not always that concerned about a credit score. But all that said, you *can* get cash advances on your credit card depending on what your interest rate is. And if that's something you are prepared to manage carefully, then it might be worth a try.

☐ **Partners:** Another way to raise a down payment is to find a partner. A lot of real estate investors miss this one. While you handle the real estate part, your partner puts the money up. Put the mortgage in your name or the partner's, and then split the profits on the sale, rents or a 50/50 refinance. To break it down more, you bring the knowledge in how to invest and the deals, and you oversee the rehab. You also set up a manager if you buy and hold or you handle selling the property. If you have positive cash flow from your rents, then you would split them with your partner. Or when you sell or refinance the property, you split 50/50. But your partner is the one making it all possible.

☐ **Seller:** Now this option is creative, but it's not overly difficult. You can find sellers who are willing to carry back from 10-30% of the purchase price as a down payment. A lender is not going to go any more than 80%. They're willing to loan 80% on any home based on the purchase price (as long as the appraisal backs up the purchase price). A lot of lenders will lend you the 80% as long as you provide an income statement that will handle the cost. And the seller likes that—especially if they've had difficulty selling, and they don't owe much on that property. They like it because they are getting their money back. They carry the second mortgage. You put it in your name, and then in 12-36 months, you refinance and take the seller out of it. They're happy, and you just purchased a property for no money down. That's a way to get a seller who will actually carry back a second mortgage

LENDING MARKETS

A man once said: The real estate business is not about real estate—it is about finance. He was right. One of the biggest hang-ups for people in real estate investing is not knowing how to finance their real estate and not knowing how loans work. I want to help you understand how a loan application flows to avoid this hang-up.

A lot of people don't know this, but in the early 1990s, the mortgage industry and the ability of the investor (or average consumer) to get loans dramatically changed. The mortgage industry went to computerized lending. And they elevated the importance of the FICO credit score, which had just come out. That made the real estate market much more liquid than it had been in the previous 100 years. Since then, three phases have developed in the loan process.

Retail Lending Market: This is where the lending market, mortgage bankers, mortgage brokers and banks intersect with the retail borrower—i.e. home buyer or multi-property (1-4 units) investor. The way this works is that we go to one of these three places to apply for a loan. The lenders underwrite the loan where we make applications according to certain criteria. The lenders that make these loans pool them together and sell them to the secondary lending market. These loans must meet certain underwriting guidelines in order to be sold to the secondary market. Occasionally you'll find a lender that will hold loans within their portfolio, called portfolio lending. Local banks will do this with you if you set up a good relationship with them so that they don't have to be concerned with the criteria.

Secondary Lending Market: This is where the quasi-government mortgage banks of Fannie Mae and Freddie Mac and a number of large private sector mortgage banks purchase these loans—typically in pools of a million dollars and up. They then repackage them in larger pools and sell them to investors in the equities market. So the retail lending market is where you and I interface primarily with getting our loans done. Then the secondary lending market is buying them and repackaging them.

Equities Lending Market: This is where pension funds, insurance companies, mutual funds, foreign investors and state governments come in. They purchase these pools or packages of loans, and they package them as mortgage securities, just like you would stock or similar things. That's why we call it the equities lending market. This is what keeps the mortgage lending industry liquid. For the foreseeable future, even 50 years from now (in my opinion), the lending market is going to be very liquid for real estate. Since the early 1990s, the underwriting system for most loans is now computerized, which makes getting approved for a loan much easier.

LOAN PROCESS TURBULENCE

The loan process can be agonizing, especially if it's your first time going about real estate investing. And sometimes, things don't go smoothly. What should have been a smooth flight, left you feeling like everything might fall through. Two tips for avoiding the following the best you can: 1. Tell the truth on your loan application! 2. Check your credit report and watch your loans!

Check out this list of real loan process issues that can come up.

• **Recent late payments on your credit report.** The lender calls, they give you a particular interest rate and tell you when they can close the loan. But then they run into a thirty-day late payment that you didn't know about. That tremendously hurts the loan process.

• **The loan officer or mortgage broker** finds out about additional debt after the application. Look at your credit report before you apply to make sure you understand what's on it.

• **Obtaining verification of rents** (if you are an investor). You need to have signed the leases that show what your income is on your particular properties.

• **Bankruptcy within the last 2 years.** That is not a good thing when you're trying to borrow money as an investor or on a personal home loan!

• **Borrower changes jobs** and goes from salary to 100%

commission income. This isn't common, but I have seen it happen. It can send the whole process into a tailspin.

- **You come up short on money at closing.** Make sure you have those liquid funds!

- **Seller loses motivation to sell.** Maybe the job transfer doesn't go through or he reconciles his marriage. That can throw you out, and you would have to go into litigation to force the seller to sell.

- **You didn't own 100% of property** as previously disclosed. Maybe you listed property on your loan application that you didn't completely own.

- **Seller does not complete repairs.** If the seller does not complete all of the repairs listed in the contract, it can hold up the process or even stop it completely.

- **Seller goes into foreclosure during escrow.** I can tell you right now, that's a major problem. Then you have to deal with the lender directly to handle that.

- **Realtor is inexperienced in investment property.** If the realtor is inexperienced in this type of property transaction, he might not report things correctly for the underwriter.

- **In an escrow company, they fail to obtain** information from lenders or insurance companies in a timely manner. I've personally experienced this—the company actually held up the closing.

- **Appraiser makes a mistake and the appraisal is wrong.** They set the value too low, and that will hold you up.

- **Inspectors do not assess minor damage correctly.** I've had an inspector do this. There was a hole in the wall that could have been patched over, which we took care of, but the loan process was held up because they said the walls were uncovered.

These might seem like small things, but they are real-life examples of things that can go wrong. I want you to know that turbulence CAN happen in a loan process. So be as prepared as you possibly can!

DO'S AND DON'TS DURING A LOAN PROCESS

When applying for a loan as a homeowner or an investor, there are certain things you want to avoid and certain things you want to make sure you do. You've applied for a loan on a particular property already. But now you're in limbo. What do you do while you wait, and maybe more importantly, what shouldn't you do? Here is a list of do's and don'ts.

- **Don't** apply for new credit. Don't apply for credit anywhere else. Don't buy a car, don't get a new credit card. Don't look at anything because it makes it seem to the lender like you're overspending!

- **Don't** pay off collections. The reason you don't want to do this is because you want to make sure that you're not changing a lot of things that the particular lender is looking at. But if they come back to you and you're not approved, you can start working on building that credit score.

- **Don't** close credit card accounts. Again, this looks like you're trying to change things to beef up your profile. Do this stuff before and after the process.

- **Don't** max out or over charge your cards. Keep a ratio of no more than 50% on each card's credit limit.

- **Don't** consolidate debt to one or two cards during the loan process. Keep everything consistent! Change things later.

- **Don't** raise red flags to the underwriter. Don't cosign on another loan. And don't move anywhere! It actually raises red flags if you change your residence during the process.

☐ **Do** join a credit watch program. I might talk more about credit scores in a future blog if there is interest.

☐ **Do** stay current on existing accounts. Don't let things slide!

☐ **Do** continue to use your credit as you normally would. Don't just shut down your credit. Keep using credit like you've typically been doing. Then it looks as though you are living life normally and handling finances in your normal way.

It's important to tread carefully in the loan process. Before and after, work hard to make that credit score awesome—but during the consideration process, you need to continue your regular rhythm of credit.

WHAT MATTERS TO AN UNDERWRITER

Knowing what matters to an underwriter can really help you prepare for getting a loan. Here are some things they look at:

1. **Credit Score:** Underwriters are looking for strong credit

scores. Check out my other two blogs about credit scores here and here.

- Anything above 720 is a $250,000 kind of score.

2. **Capacity:** Be prepared to share just about everything. Underwriters want to see all income and assets documented—as well as have an idea of how you're living.

- Full Document Loan

- DTI (debt-to-income ratio) of 28% is ideal. (for mortgage, 36% for all)

- Documents—taxes, pay stubs, VOE (verification of employment), VOA (verification of accounts)

3. **Collateral:** Collateral is definitely something that matters to underwriters. This is the protection. Without it, the institution is vulnerable. Study up on mortgages and borrowing before moving ahead. You'll want to know as much as the underwriter when it comes to this field.

- LTV: Loan-to-value ratio. (ideally high–80% or more, determined by appraisal first mortgage 80%)

- To 90% with Mortgage Insurance

- Most borrowers do 80/10/10

- For higher LTV ratios you can do 80/15, 75/20 or even a 75/25 for a 100% loan

4. **Character:** Beyond all of the previous areas, underwriters want to see strong character! Be someone they can trust.

- Time on Job: Minimum of 2 years. Bring VOE.

- Time at Residence: About 2 years.

–   Your Age (50 is better than 30.)

–   DTI: Get your debt-to-income ratio under control—not more than 40%!

–   Assets: Down payment + 6 months reserves. Bring VOA.

–   Seasoned Funds 60 days

–   Two Years Tax Returns

–   Number of properties owned

–   Last two months of pay stubs

PROPERTY CHECKLIST

Once you've found a property you like, don't jump. Learn how to properly inspect and improve! Find a quality professional inspector, and get a written report. You are looking for properties that can be *lipsticked*, not rebuilt. I've made a ton of mistakes in real estate. But this list is what I follow, and I think it will help you get focused on a property. Think about the house in these terms, and you will set up the right boundaries.

What to inspect: A property's interior

☐ Water damage. Check the roof and the plumbing to make sure nothing is damaged!

☐ Lead-based paint. This will require treatment and a repaint, so be aware.

☐ Windows. I once looked at a place with terrible

windows. They wouldn't open! Make sure to check if they are operational.

☐ Appliances. Check for age and functionality.

☐ Cabinets/Counters. Check for serious aesthetic injuries and calculate that into your cost.

☐ Plumbing. Make sure to scope this out well. Check for leaks and flush toilets.

☐ Electrical. Do all the plugs work? How is electrical paneling interior?

☐ Heating/Cooling. Make sure this is working! This can be a pain to find out later.

What to improve: A property's interior

☐ Remove all debris. This is the easy step!

☐ Clean everything. Hire a thorough service or if you're just beginning, get your friends involved!

☐ Paint!!! This can be the best and quickest refresher. Stay neutral generally. Make sure to use a color palette, color board, and get a couple of opinions on your choice. Take a look in your area, and see what colors model homes are using!

☐ New floors. Again, an amazing refresher. Find carpet and tile that fits your color board.

☐ New bath and kitchen faucets. Often overlooked, but necessary. I saw a place that had poor bathroom faucets, and it caused all kinds of stains from leaking around the sink.

☐ Refurbish or replace kitchen and bath cabinets. Cabinets show wear heavily. Make sure these are fresh, and the whole place will feel new!

What to inspect: A property's exterior

☐ Roof. Is there life left? Look for sagging, discoloration, etc.

☐ Chimney. I once looked at a property with 17 small chimneys that all needed replacement. Check them out!

☐ Siding. What kind? Does it need covered or replaced?

☐ Services. What is the setup here? Check sewer, water meter, electric panel and gas. Is it functional?

☐ Foundation. Look for cracked slab that needs leveling and bad beams.

☐ Termites. Such a pain. Look out.

☐ Septic tanks. Make sure everything is working here.

What to improve: A property's exterior

☐ Landscaping. Again if you are new, you can get your family to help here. Treat overgrown bushes, plant new flowers and lay fresh mulch.

☐ Shutters. An easy rejuvenating touch for the outside appeal. Find a safe but attractive color, and go with it.

☐ Paint. Along with the shutters, treat trim, front door, garage door…. If it can be livened up easily, liven it up.

☐ New front door. Make sure no drafts are getting in.

☐ New exterior trim lights. This will help the place sell again and again. Keep it bright. RECOMMENDED READING

RECOMMENDED READING

I have read thousands upon thousands of books in my lifetime—all in an effort to bring value to the market! The authors of these books have all had a profound impact on my life. I have used direct quotes from some of them. But all of them have in some way shaped my thinking on the issue of wealth building. Behind the words in this book are the authors of countless others who have inspired me.

Business

Pour Your Heart into It: How Starbucks Built a Company One Cup at a Time by Howard Schultz

The Secrets to Writing a Successful Business Plan: A Pro Shares a Step-By-Step Guide to Creating a Plan That Gets Results by Hal Shelton

Tribes: We Need You to Lead Us by Set Godin

Platform: Get Noticed in a Noisy World by Michael Hyatt

Getting Things Done: The Art of Stress-Free Productivity by David Allen

Start Your Own Business by Entrepreneur Press

God @ Work: Developing Ministers in the Marketplace, Vol. 2 by Rich Marshall

What is your One Sentence?: How to Be Heard in the Age of Short Attention Spans by Mimi Goss

Nuts: Southwest Airlines' Crazy Recipe for Business and Personal Success by Kevin and Jackie Freiberg

The Art of Leadership, 4th Edition by George Manning and Kent Curtis

Putting the One Minute Manager to Work by Kenneth Blanchard, Ph.D. and Robert Lorber, Ph.D.

Bootstrapping Your Business: Start and Grow a Successful Company with Almost No Money by Greg Gianforte with Marcus Gibson

Own Your Own Corporation by Garrett Sutton, Esq.

Anointed for Business: How to Use Your Influence in the Marketplace to Change the World by Ed Silvoso

Business Plans for Dummies by Paul Tiffany and Steven D. Peterson

The One-Minute Manager by Kenneth Blanchard, Ph.D. and Spencer Johnson, M.D.

Good to Great: Why Some Companies Make the Leap... and Others Don't by Jim Collins

Jewish Wisdom for Business Success by Levi Brackman and Sam Jaffe

Finance for Non-Financial Managers and Small Business Owners by Lawrence W. Tuller

How to Buy and Sell a Business: How You Can Win in the Business Quadrant by Garrett Sutton, Esq.

The E Myth Revisited: Why Most Small Businesses Don't Work and What to Do About It by Michael E. Gerber

Managing Human Resources: Productivity, Quality of Work Life, Profits, Ninth Edition by Wayne F. Cascio

How to Start, Run, and Stay in Business by Gregory F. Kishel and Patricia Gunter Kishel

The ABC's of Writing Winning Business Plans, How to Prepare a Business Plan that Others Will Want to Read—and Invest In by Garrett Sutton Esq."

The ABC's of Building a Business Team That Wins: The Invisible Code of Honor That Takes Ordinary People and Turns them into a Championship Team by Blair Singer

Operations Management, Processes and Supply Chains, Tenth Edition by Lee J. Krajewski, Larry P. Ritzman and Manoj K. Malhotra

The Secrets of Facilitation, the SMART Guide to Getting Results with Groups, New and Revised by Michael Wilkinson

Annual Editions: Marketing 12/13, Thirty-Fifth Edition edited by John E. Richardson and Nisreen N. Bahnan

The Plan-As-You-Go Business Plan by Tim Berry

How to Prepare and Present a Business Plan by Joseph R. Mancuso

Valuation: The Art and Science of Corporate Investment Decisions, Second Edition by Sheridan Titman and John D. Martin

A Preface to Marketing Management, 13th Edition by J. Paul Peter and James H. Donnelly, Jr.

Corporate Finance, Core Principles and Applications, Third Edition by Stephen A. Ross, Randolph W. Westerfield, Jeffrey F. Jaffe and Bradford D. Jordan

Applications in Business Communication: A Systems Approach by D. Jackie Hartman and Brenda Ogden

Learning from the Future: Competitive Foresight Scenarios by Liam Fahey and Robert M. Randall

How to Measure Anything: Finding the Value of 'Intangibles' in Business by Douglas W. Hubbard

IT Savvy: What Top Executives Must Know to Go from Pain to Gain by Peter Weill and Jeanne W. Ross

Crossing the Chasm: Marketing and Selling Disruptive Products to Mainstream Customers by Geoffrey A. Moore

Business Model Generation by Alexander Osterwalder and Yves Pigneur

Strengths Finder 2.0 by Tom Rath

Venture Capital for Dummies by Nicole Gravagna Ph.D. and Peter K. Adams, MBA

Managerial Economics: A Problem Solving Approach, 2nd Edition by Luke M. Froeb and Brian T. McCann

Essentials of Investments, Ninth Edition by Zvi Bodie, Alex Kane and Alan J. Marcus

Own Your Own Corporation: Why the Rich Own Their Own Companies and Everyone Else Works For Them by Garrett Sutton, Esq.

Personal Finance/Inspirational

24 Essential Lessons for Investment Success by William J. O'Neil

Retire Rich: How to Plan a Secure Financial Future by David Evan Morse

The World's Greatest Wealth Builder by Carleton H. Sheets

Multiple Streams of Income: How to Generate a Lifetime of Unlimited Wealth by Robert G. Allen

Start Late, Finish Rich: A No-Fail Plan for Achieving Financial Freedom at Any Age by David Bach

The Laws of Money: 5 Timeless Secrets to Get Out and Stay Out of Financial Trouble by Suze Orman

Multiple Streams of Internet Income: How Ordinary People Make

Extraordinary Money Online by Robert G. Allen

The Secret by Rhonda Byrne

The One-Minute Millionaire: The Enlightened Way to Wealth by Mark Victor Hansen and Robert G. Allen

Rags to Retirement: Stories from People Who Retired Well on Much Less Than You'd Think by Gail Liberman and Alan Lavine

Getting Everything You Can out of All You've Got by Jay Abraham

You're Fifty—Now What? Investing for the Second Half of Your Life by Charles R. Schwab

Finding Meaning in the Second Half of Life: How to Finally, Really Grow Up by James Hollis, Ph.D.

The Little Money Book by David Boyle

Your Money or Your Life: Transforming Your Relationship with Money and Achieving Financial Independence by Joe Dominguez and Vicki Robin

More than Enough: The 10 Keys to Changing Your Financial Destiny by Dave Ramsey

Ninety Days to Financial Fitness by Don and Joan German

Accounting: What the Numbers Mean by David Marshall

Secrets of Jewish Wealth Revealed by Celso Cukierkorn

End of the Fed by Ron Paul

Irrational Exuberance by Robert J. Shiller

MONEY Master the Game: 7 Simple Steps to Financial Freedom by Tony Robbins

Organize Your Mind, Organize Your Life: Train Your Brain to Get More Done in Less Time by Margaret Moore and Paul Hammerness

Outliers: The Story of Success by Malcolm Gladwell

Please Understand Me II by David Keirsey

Rebounders: How Winners Pivot From Stepback to Success by Rick Newman

The Crash Course: The Unsustainable Future of Our Economy, Energy, and Environment by Chris Martenson

The Goal: A Process of Ongoing Improvement by Eliyahu M. Goldratt and Jeff Cox

The Millionaire Next Door: The Surprising Secrets of America's Wealthy by Thomas J. Stanley Ph.D. and William D. Danko Ph.D.

The Motivation Manifesto by Brendon Burchard

Thou Shall Prosper: Ten Commandments for Making Money by Daniel Lapin

'Yes' or 'No': The Guide to Better Decisions by Spencer Johnson, M.D.

The Tipping Point: How Little Things Can Make a Big Difference by Malcolm Gladwell

Creating Wealth: Retire in Ten Years Using Allen's Seven Principles of Wealth, Revised and Updated by Robert G. Allen

Do What You Love, the Money Will Follow by Marsha Sinetar

The Art of the Start: The Time-Tested, Battle-Hardened Guide for Anyone Starting Anything by Guy Kawasaki

The New Rules of Money: 80 Simple Strategies for Financial Success Today by Ric Edelman

The 4-Hour Workweek: Escape 9-5, Live Anywhere, and Join the New Rich by Timothy Ferriss

Buckets of Money: How to Retire in Comfort and Safety by Raymond J. Lucia, CFP with Dale Fetherling

The Secret of Shelter Island: Money and What Matters by Alexander Green

Wealth 101: Getting What You Want—Enjoying What You've Got by John-Roger and Peter McWilliams

The Number: A Completely Different Way to Think About the Rest of Your Life by Lee Eisenberg

Your Credit Score: How to Fix, Improve, and Protect the 3-Digit Number that Shapes Your Financial Future by Liz Pulliam Weston

Missed Fortune 101: A Starter Kit to Becoming a Millionaire by Douglas R. Andrew

How to Retire Happy, Wild, and Free: Retirement Wisdom That You Won't Get From Your Financial Advisor by Ernie J. Zelinski

Making Money: Winning the Battle for Middle-Class Financial Success by Howard Ruff

How to Retire Early and Live Well with Less Than A Million Dollars by Gillette Edmunds

Ready... Set ... Retire!: Financial Strategies for the Rest of Your Life by Raymond J. Lucia, CFP with Dale Fetherling

Live Long and Prosper: Invest in Your Happiness, Health, and Wealth for Retirement and Beyond by Steve Vernon

The Guerilla Guide to Credit Repair: How to Find Out What's Wrong With Your Credit Rating—And How To Fix It by Todd Bierman and

Nathaniel Wice

Guide to Investing: What the Rich Invest In, That the Poor and Middle Class Do Not! by Robert T. Kiyosaki with Sharon L. Lechter, C.P.A

Live It Up without Outliving Your Money: 10 Steps to a Perfect Retirement Portfolio by Paul Merriman

Younger Next Year: A Guide to Living like 50 until You're 80 and Beyond by Chris Crowley and Henry S. Lodge, M.D.

Retire on Less Than You Think: The New York Times Guide to Planning Your Financial Future by Fred Brock

Rich Dad Poor Dad: What the Rich Teach Their Kids about Money—that the Poor and Middle Class Do Not! by Robert T. Kiyosaki with Sharon L. Lechter

Rich Dad's Cashflow Quadrant: Rich Dad's Guide to Financial Freedom by Robert T. Kiyosaki with Sharon L. Lechter

Rich Dad's Guide to Becoming Rich without Cutting Up Your Credit Cards: Turn "Bad Debt" into "Good Debt" by Robert T. Kiyosaki with Sharon L. Lechter

OPM Other People's Money: How to Attract Other People's Money for Your Investments—the Ultimate Leverage by Michael A. Lechter, Esq

Retire Young Retire Rich: How to Get Rich Quickly and Stay Rich Forever! by Robert T. Kiyosaki with Sharon L. Lechter

Your Retirement Your Way: Why It Takes More Than Money to Live Your Dream by Albert Bernstein, LCSW, and John Trauth, M.B.A.

Unlimited Power by Anthony Robbins

Retire and Thrive: Remarkable People, Age 50-Plus, Share Their Creative, Productive and Profitable Retirement Strategies by Robert K.

Otterbourg

Real Estate

The ABC's of Real Estate Investing: The Secrets of Finding Hidden Profits Most Investors Miss by Ken McElroy

Real Estate Riches: How to Become Rich Using Your Banker's Money by Dolf De Roos, Ph.D.

Real Estate Loop-Holes: Secrets of Successful Real Estate Investing by Diane Kennedy, C.P.A. and Garrett Sutton, Esq.

Successful Real Estate Investing: How to Avoid the 75 Most Costly Mistakes Every Investor Makes by Robert Shemin

The Beginner's Guide to Real Estate Investing by Gary W. Eldred, Ph.D.

How to be a Quick Turn Real Estate Millionaire: Make Fast Cash with No Money, Credit, or Previous Experience by Ron LeGrand

The Complete Idiot's Guide to Making Money with Rental Properties by Brian F. Edwards, Casey Edwards, and Susannah Craig-Edwards

How to Rent Vacation Properties by Owner: The Complete Guide to Buy, Manage, Furnish, Rent, Maintain and Advertise your Vacation Rental Investment by Christine Hrib Karpinski

Successful Real Estate Investing in a Boom or Bust Market by Larry B. Loftis, Esq.

The Real Estate Fast Track: How to Create a $5,000 to $50,000 per Month Real Estate Cash Flow by David Finkel

Entrepreneur's Great Big Book on Real Estate Investing: Everything You Need to Know to Create Wealth in Real Estate by Stuart Leland Rider

Real Estate for Boomers and Beyond: Exploring the Costs, Choices and Changes for Your Next Move by Tom Kelly

Buy and Hold: 7 Steps to a Real Estate Fortune by David Schumacher, Ph.D.

Bubbles, Booms and Busts: Make Money in Any Real Estate Market by Blanche Evans

From 0 to 130 Properties in 3.5 Years by Steve McKnight

Tips and Traps When Mortgage Hunting by Robert Irwin

Be a Real Estate Millionaire: Secrets Strategies for Lifetime Wealth Today by Dean Graziosi

The Coming Crash in the Housing Market: 10 Things You can Do Now to Protect Your Most Valuable Investment by John R. Talbott

Insider Secrets to Financing Your Real Estate Investments: What Every Real Estate Investor Needs to Know About Finding and Financing Your Next Deal by Frank Gallinelli

What Every Real Estate Investor Needs to Know About Cash Flow... And 36 Other Key Financial Measures by Frank Gallinelli

Investing in Real Estate, Third Edition by Andrew McLean and Gary W. Eldred, Ph.D.

The Weekend Millionaire's Secrets to Investing in Real Estate by Mike Summey and Roger Dawson

Real Estate Investing from A to Z: The Most Comprehensive, Practical, and Readable Guide to Investing Profitably in Real Estate, Third Edition by William H. Pivar

Getting Started in Real Estate Investing, by Second Edition Michael C. Thomsett and Jean Freestone Thomsett

What No One Ever Tells You About Investing in Real Estate: Real-Life Advice from 101 Successful Investors by Robert J. Hill II, Esq.

All Real Estate Is Local: What You Need to Know to Profit in Real Estate—In a Buyer's and a Seller's Market by David Lereah

Trump Strategies for Real Estate: Billionaire Lessons for the Small Investor by George H. Ross with Andrew James McLean

Investing in Duplexes, Triplexes and Quads: The Fastest and Safest Way to Real Estate Wealth by Larry B. Loftis, Esq.

Buy, Rent and Sell: How to Profit by Investing in Residential Real Estate by Robert Irwin

Start Small, Profit Big in Real Estate: Fixer Jay's 2-Year Plan for Building Wealth—Starting from Scratch! by Jay P. DeCima

The Landlord's Kit: A Complete Set of Ready-to-Use Forms, Letters, and Notices to Increase Profits, Take Control, and Eliminate the Hassles of Property Management by Jeffrey Taylor

The Millionaire Real Estate Investor by Gary Keller with Dave Jenks and Jay Papasan

Flipping Properties: Generate Instant Cash Profits in Real Estate by William Bronchick and Robert Dahlstrom

Value Investing in Real Estate by Gary W. Eldred, Ph.D.

The Unofficial Guide to Real Estate Investing by Martin Stone and Spencer Strauss

Real Estate Debt Can Make You Rich: What You Owe Today Is What You Will Be Worth Tomorrow by Steve Dexter

Timing the Real Estate Market by Craig Hall

The Insider's Guide to Making Money in Real Estate: Smart Steps to

Building Your Wealth through Property by Dolf De Roos, Ph.D. and Diane Kennedy, CPA

Maverick Real Estate Investing: The Art of Buying and Selling Properties like Trump, Zell, Simon, and the World's Greatest Land Owners by Steve Bergsman

The Smart Money Guide to Real Estate Investing by Gerri Willis

Nothing Down: A Proven Program That Shows You How to Buy Real Estate with Little or No Money Down by Robert G. Allen

Streetwise Investing in Rental Housing: A Detailed Strategy for Financial Independence by H. Roger Neal

All About Real Estate Investing: The Easy Way to Get Started, Second Edition by William Benke and Joseph M. Fowler

Investing in a Vacation Home for Pleasure and Profit by James. H. Boykin

Unlimited Riches: Making Your Fortune in Real Estate Investing by Robert Shemin

How to Get Started in Real Estate Investing by Robert Irwin

How to Find Hidden Real Estate Bargains: For Home Buyers and Investors Looking to Uncover a Wealth of Opportunities by Robert Irwin

5 Magic Paths to Making a Fortune in Real Estate: Learn How to Buy, Renovate, and Sell by James Lumley

The Real Estate Millionaire: How to Invest in Rental Markets and Make a Fortune by Boaz Gilad and Susanne Gilad

Make More Money Investing in Multi-units: A Step-by-Step Guide to Profiting from Apartment Buildings by Gregory D. Warr

How to Make $1,000,000 in Real Estate in Three Years Starting With

No Cash by Tyler G. Hicks

Rich Dad's Real Estate Advantages: Tax and Legal Secrets of Successful Real Estate Investors by Sharon L. Lechter and Garrett Sutton Esq.

How to Make Big Money in Real Estate by Tyler G. Hicks

How to Buy and Sell Apartment Buildings by Eugene E. Vollucci

The Complete Guide to Buying and Selling Apartment Buildings by Steve Berges

Make Millions by Buying Small Apartment Properties in Your Spare Time by Brian K. Friedman

How a Second Home Can Be Your Best Investment by Tom Kelly and John Tuccillo

Building Wealth One House at a Time by John W. Schaub

2 Years to a Million in Real Estate by Matthew A. Martinez

Building Wealth: From Rags to Riches through Real Estate by Russ Whitney

Unlimited Real Estate Profit: Create Wealth and Build a Financial Fortress through Today's Real Estate Investing by Mark Stephan Garrison, M.B.A. and Paula Tripp-Garrison

Are You Missing the Real Estate Boom? Why Home Values and Other Real Estate Investments Will Climb through the End of the Decade—and How to Profit From Them by David Lereah

Successful Real Estate Investing, a Practical Guide to Profits for the Small Investor by Peter G. Miller

Getting Started in Rental Income by Michael C. Thomsett

Secrets of a Millionaire Real Estate Investor by Robert Shemin, Esq.

Social Impact

A Good African Story: How a Small Company Built a Global Coffee Brand by Andrew Rugasira

A Billion Bootstraps: Microcredit, Barefoot Banking, and the Business Solution for Ending Poverty by Philip Smith and Eric Thurman

Nonprofit Essentials: Effective Donor Relations by Janet L. Hedrick

Microfinance for Bankers and Investors: Understanding the Opportunities and Challenges of the Market at the Bottom of the Pyramid by Elisabeth Rhyne

Dead Aid: Why Aid Is Not Working and How There is a Better Way for Africa by Dambisa Moyo

Sustainable Banking with the Poor: Microfinance Handbook, an Institutional and Financial Perspective by Joanna Ledgerwood

Stock Market

Investing with Exchange-Traded Funds Made Easy: Higher Returns with Lower Costs—Do It Yourself Strategies without Paying Fund Managers by Marvin Appel

24 Essential Lessons for Investment Success by William J. O'Neil

Jesse Livermore World's Greatest Stock Trader by Richard Smitten

How to Make Money in Stocks: A Winning System in Good Times or Bad, Third Edition—Completely Updated by William J. O'Neil

Jim Cramer's Real Money: Sane Investing in an Insane World by James J. Cramer

Trading Rules: Strategies for Success by William F. Eng

Americans Became Successful Investors—and How You Can Too by Ric Edelman

How I Made $2,000,000 in the Stock Market by Nicholas Darvas

Ordinary, People, Extraordinary Wealth: The 8 Secrets of How 5,000 Ordinary Americans Became Successful Investors by Ric Edelman

How to Make Money in Stocks: A Winning System in Good Times or Bad by William J. O'Neil

The Travels of a T-Shirt in the Global Economy: An Economist Examines the Markets, Power, and Politics of World Trade by Pietra Rivoli

Aftershock: Protect Yourself and Profit in the Next Global Financial Meltdown by David Wiedemer, Robert A. Wiedemer and Cindy S. Spitzer

Rich Dad's Guide to Investing by Robert Kiyosaki

The (Mis) Behavior of Markets: A Fractal View of Risk, Ruin and Reward by Richard L. Hudson

The Greatest Trade Ever: The Behind-the-Scenes Story of How John Paulson Defied Wall Street and Made Financial History by Gregory Zuckerman

The How to Make Money in Stocks Complete Investing System: Your Ultimate Guide to Winning in Good Times and Bad by William O'Neil

The Permanent Portfolio: Harry Browne's Long-Term Investment Strategy by Craig Rowland and J.M. Lawson

Trading in the Shadow of Smart Money by Gavin Holmes

Learn to Earn: A Beginner's Guide to the Basics of Investing and Business by Peter Lynch and John Rothchild

A GIFT FOR YOU

If you are looking for a change in your life or if you are seeking a peace that is found through a personal relationship with a loving God, then He is ready and willing to help you—right now and right where you are.

Salvation is a gift that is made available to those who repent, believe, and confess that Jesus is Lord. Jesus died and rose from the dead to save mankind (Acts 16:31; Romans 10:9-10). This gift cannot be received through good deeds or by simply being a good person (Ephesians 2:8, 1 Timothy 1:9). It's received by faith—by believing and acting on God's Word concerning salvation.

Pray this prayer aloud from your heart:

> *Heavenly Father, I come to You in the name of Jesus. Your Word says, "…Whoever calls on the name of the Lord shall be saved" (Acts 2:21). I am calling on You.*
>
> *I pray and ask Jesus to come into my heart and be Lord and Savior over my life. According to Romans 10:9-10, "…If you confess with your mouth the Lord Jesus and believe in your heart that God has raised Him from the dead, you will be saved."*
>
> *I do that now. I confess Jesus as my Lord, and I believe in my heart that God raised Him from the dead.*

If you have prayed this prayer, welcome to the family of God! Share your good news with us at www.harrisonhouse.com and let us know what God has done in your life.

For more information about Billy Epperhart, a listing of additional teaching materials, or to enjoy his weekly financial blog, visit www.billyepperhart.com. He also can be reached via info@billyepperhart.com or (720) 416-4600.